Fires in the Bathroom

From the reviews of *Fires in the Bathroom*

"In *Fires in the Bathroom*... students turn the tables on adults, and tell them how to do their jobs." – *New York Times*

"An important book... a powerful critique of American teaching... *Fires in the Bathroom* should find a place in any professional development library... The student voices give its advice... an authenticity and a sincerity that advice books for teachers often lack... A powerful and compelling document... A major contribution." – *Teachers College Record*

"*Fires in the Bathroom* doles out practical advice... [in] an unusual... effort to tap the opinions of American high school students... Students get a rare opportunity to voice their opinions about what works and what doesn't." – *Los Angeles Times*

"This book turns the student-teacher relationship upside down... Suggests ways to deepen the unspoken bond between students and teachers." – *Chicago Tribune*, Editor's Choice

"This chance to hear the authentic voice of students... should not be overlooked by anyone involved in teen education." – *Publishers Weekly*

"Thoughtful and articulate... offer[s] insights about a range of school-related subjects, including classroom behavior, student motivation, and learning style." – *Teacher Magazine*

"*Fires in the Bathroom* is a must for everyone concerned about our children and our schools... A wealth of information that can be put to immediate use... Treat yourself to this powerful new tool!" – *Connections Magazine*

Fires in the Bathroom

Advice for Teachers from High School Students

Kathleen Cushman

and the students of What Kids Can Do

with an introduction by Lisa Delpit

THE NEW PRESS

New York ▪ London

Requests for permission to reproduce selections from this book should
be mailed to: Permissions Department, The New Press, 120 Wall Street,
31st floor, New York, NY 10005

Published in the United States by The New Press, New York, 2003
Distributed by Two Rivers Distribution

ISBN 978-1-56584-802-3 (HC)
ISBN 978-1-56584-996-9 (PB)
CIP data available

Book design by Sandra Delany.

The New Press publishes books that promote and enrich public
discussion and understanding of the issues vital to our democracy
and to a more equitable world. These books are made possible by the
enthusiasm of our readers; the support of a committed group of
donors, large and small; the collaboration of our many partners in the
independent media and the not-for-profit sector; booksellers, who often
hand-sell New Press books; librarians; and above all by our authors.

www.thenewpress.com

Printed in the United States of America

24 23 22 21 20 19 18 17 16

This book is dedicated

to all the students whose voices are still unheard

and all of those whose voices helped create it

Alexis	*Luis*
Andres	*Mahogany*
Barbara	*Marcos*
Bosung	*Maribel*
Brian	*Mika*
Cynthia	*Montoya*
Daryl	*Murilo*
Diana	*Nai*
Donnel	*Nathan*
Elaine	*Pedro*
Hilary	*Porsche*
Jae Yoon	*Rafael*
Javier	*Sam*
Jin Fen	*Sandy*
Karen	*Tiffany*
Kirandeep	*Tsugumi*
Krishneel	*Vance*
Latia	*Veronica*
Lauraliz	*Ximena*
Luciana	*Yuri*

Contents

Preface

"AND THEN THEY SET FIRES IN THE BATHROOM,
WHILE SHE WAS TRYING TO BE SO FRIENDLY."

It's a safe bet that in random high schools all over the United States, some kid has just set the bathroom wastebasket on fire. And deep down, all of us know why.

Anyone who has made it out of their teens most likely remembers the feelings of anonymity and captivity that even the best high schools can convey. Whether in huge urban warehouses, sprawling suburban campuses, or newly consolidated rural schools, teachers with more than 125 students a day can't help but focus the majority of their attention on only the most urgent cases.

In such settings, order trumps most other institutional aims. To keep the place running smoothly, students' behavior becomes more important than their understanding, acquiescence more valued than inquiry. In pursuit of order, school and classroom rules routinely supplant the disarray of kids' questions, objections, suggestions, and problems. High school becomes something done *to* kids, not *by* kids. This is the way it works; this is the way it has always worked.

Against this backdrop, the voices of the students who helped write this book took on even more importance to What Kids Can Do, Inc. (WKCD), the new nonprofit organization that asked me to gather teenagers' advice for an audience of teachers and the public. Based in Providence, Rhode Island, WKCD researches and makes public the work and learning of adolescents around the United States via its website and also through networks of others who care about or work with youth. For this book project, WKCD won support from MetLife Foundation, whose Supporting New Teachers Initiative recognizes how much new teachers could learn from students—if only given the chance.

With two million new teachers needed over the next decade and 60 percent of beginning teachers quitting the profession within their first five years, advice from the classroom could not be more important. Research shows that too many schools across the country suffer from a persistent divide, one pitting teachers and students against each other. In a 2001 national survey, 65 percent of students agreed with the statement, "My teachers don't understand me," and 33 percent of the teachers reported inadequate preparation to reach students with backgrounds different from their own.[*]

In this climate, I set out to collect what would become sheaves of interviews and writing from forty students in New York City, Providence, and the San Francisco Bay Area. Through school connections made during years of education writing, I found ordinary students who reflected the faces and backgrounds of their diverse student populations. Some had moved from typical big-city schools into small schools; others had dropped out altogether before returning to class. Several performed well academically, but many struggled. Twenty were recent immigrants, English-language learners in a special class at a large California high school. Another half dozen spoke no English at home but took regular classes at school. Whenever I found students who agreed to participate, I asked whether they could interest a friend in coming, too.

Except for the class of English-language learners, we met in small groups of three to five students, usually on weekends and during school vacations. Each group worked for at least three sessions of three to five hours, and we paid students for their time at an hourly rate comparable to that of undergraduate research assistants.

From their short biographies (pages 197 to 199) and their words throughout this book, a vivid mosaic emerges of the individual narratives these students

[*] *The MetLife Survey of the American Teacher.* New York City: MetLife, Inc., 2000 and 2001.

brought to our discussions, debate, and analysis. As diverse a group in ethnicity and academic record as their schoolmates in the cities where they live, these young messengers realize well that most of their teachers do not share their background. Their advice also recognizes the differences among themselves: Every high school student is unique, making the teacher's job even harder.

Yet strikingly, their daily encounters with teachers ring true across the board—not just for students of color and language minorities like themselves, but equally for their more privileged peers. As they trade wisdom on how to navigate high school, they invariably strike the same chords kids everywhere sound when they let down their guard to recount their school experiences.

"Socially, kids hate you if you succeed too much," observes Mika, whose strict Jamaican parents demand the highest achievement from her. "It's like: 'Shut up! Why do you have to rub it in my face that you know and I don't!' I didn't learn that until it was too late, and then I completely shut up in class." Alexis, who has shuttled through three New York City high schools, elaborates: "Intimidation is the key. Teenagers care about what other people think of them, and so they feel intimidated."

They speak of their need to be known well but to maintain boundaries and privacy. They crave respect from adults, feeling retaliatory rage when humiliated or ignored. "Kids want to learn," in one Harlem student's words, and they hunger for the power to shape their own futures. They know their lives are in flux, and when things go wrong, they want someone to help without shaming them. As Alexis points out, "Teachers need to make allowance for the fact that we change from year to year and even from week to week."

Throughout their work on this book, students showed enormous appreciation for the teachers who helped them learn. Though they offer plenty of criticism and advice, they testify time after time to a teacher's power to change their minds and their lives. They respond with real attachment and respect when a teacher believes in them, offering support through difficulties. Maribel's favorite teacher at her large Providence high school "is always willing to talk and can get you interested by asking questions." Alexis describes her math teacher: "He won't let you give up." And they observe that sometimes a good teacher helps them learn just by treating them with warmth and understanding. "She would find times outside of the classroom to ask me how I was doing, and to let me know that I could go to her if I needed anything at all," says Tiffany about a teacher who recognized the difficulty of being a black student in a largely white school. Veronica, a fifteen-year-old from Oakland, says of her biology teacher: "He has changed our lives forever."

As originally conceived, this book would have devoted a chapter to each of the key academic areas, offering students' insights on how to teach them most effectively. But as the torrent of student voices mounted with each work session, we realized the mistake of that assumption. Our groups offered surprisingly little critique of curriculum and assessment. They focused more on the relationships that made learning possible.

Might listening carefully to these students change high schools enough so kids would no longer set fires in the bathroom? We know instinctively that teachers, as with physicians and attorneys, perform best when they not only know their material well but notice and respond sensitively to the people they serve. But faced with the ever-shifting needs and opinions of adolescents, a teacher might easily despair of ever hitting the delicate balance these student co-authors say they want: adult authority and guidance mixed with a healthy measure of flexibility.

Without genuine dialogue, such an aim remains elusive. In organizing students' words into the following chapters, I tried to focus their diverse perspectives, with the goal of fostering better communication. In the narrative voice, "we" indicates student consensus on their advice, and I revert to the third person when summarizing or interpreting their responses. Kids' observations, at times blunt and irreverent, appear here unedited, with an occasional translation for those of us not cool enough to understand. For the sake of authenticity, I chose not to exclude suggestions that seasoned teachers would agree are impractical.

Above all, this book aims to foster a teacher's habit of paying close attention to what students say, whether they speak through words or actions. As Lauraliz, a quiet and careful seventeen-year-old from the Bronx, reminds us: "I been looking for a teacher I can talk to, and I think I found that teacher. I don't really know how to approach him yet, but when I need to talk about something, I'll find a way."

One day, after a long and animated work session, I asked the students around our table, "Has anyone ever asked you questions like these before?" They paused to think, then every head shook no.

This book, I hope, will help to right that silence.

Kathleen Cushman
Harvard, Massachusetts
September 2002

Introduction

by Lisa Delpit

"WANTED: ONE TEACHER. MUST BE ABLE TO LISTEN, EVEN WHEN MAD."

Must have a sense of humor; must not make students feel bad about themselves; must be fair and not treat some students better than others; must know how to make schoolwork interesting; must keep some students from picking on others; must let students take a break sometimes; must not jump to conclusions; must let students know them; must get to know students; must encourage students when they have a hard time; must tell students if they do a good job or try really hard; must not scream; must not call home unless it's really important; must smile; must help students with their problems *if* they ask; must not talk about students to other people; must be patient; must really know what they are teaching; if it's a lady, it would be good if she is pretty.

This is the job description created by a group of eighth- and ninth-graders when, during the first two weeks of school, I filled in for an absent teacher at a predominantly African American charter school at which I served as a consultant. Not having a lesson plan and not knowing much about the subject at hand, I decided to have the students think about what they wanted in a teacher. I was not really surprised at their ability to articulate their perspectives—I have known for many years that the fastest way to find out about the work of a teacher is to ask the students—but in my haste to provide instructional inservice for the teachers or administrative help for the principal, I had forgotten about the need to really listen to the students.

That is what this book is about. It is full of the exceptional wisdom about teaching gleaned by listening to students. It is about seeing students as complete human beings, with minds, hearts, and souls, rather than as test scores to be raised. It is about adults taking on the role not only of instructor but of trusted elder, guide, coach, leader, and perhaps sometimes friend.

In my work at the charter school, I learned and relearned what was needed in education. I spent every day at the school. I was not officially teacher or administrator. Indeed, one of the students introduced me to a new student as "the mother of the school," an appellation I subsequently wore with great pride. As school "mother," I roamed the common area, the halls, and the classrooms, looking to de-escalate potentially explosive situations, removing one or more disruptive students from a classroom for a conversation, providing a hug or a shoulder for a sad or angry child, assisting a teacher in explaining a complicated concept, modeling an interesting instructional strategy when I noticed lethargy setting in, "handling" discipline problems, finding lost bookbags, calling parents for sick children, and so on. It was in that role that I became reacquainted with the power of children's thoughts about the educational enterprise. With one eye on who these young people are at the moment and one eye on what they have the potential to become in the future, the amount of intellectual energy it takes for adults to solve school problems with integrity, thoughtfulness, and caring is enormous.

There were so many moments during my time at that school for which this book could have been a resource. There was the sixth grader who spent more time put out of class than learning in it. Bryant (not his real name) told me that he was sick of his classmates because they were dumb and didn't know what they should know in sixth grade. That was why he always called them stupid idiots and called out answers to the teacher's questions. It would have been easy to dismiss him as just a rude young man, as most of his teachers had done. After talking with me for a while, though, he revealed that he felt he had not been invited into the class by either the students or the teachers. We talked about what people who were successful in the world knew about working with other people and how it was important to make people feel good about themselves if you wanted them to feel good about you.

I can't say that it was a complete success story, but Bryant was able to feel more included. Gradually some of his classmates began to draw him into their groups; to his credit, he went to one of the other adults in the school whom he thought embodied the traits he wanted to develop and asked her to become his "mentor."

One morning in another, more dramatic moment, I was called into the office as soon as I arrived. The principal had her hands full with a budgetary emergency and there was a major problem in one of the pre-algebra classes that had had three inexperienced teachers since the beginning of the school year. The students had apparently walked out of the recently hired math teacher's classroom en masse and refused to go back in. I walked to the classroom wondering how I would handle the situation. I found the students all sitting in the common space outside the classroom and the teacher wandering around inside the classroom, occasionally coming to the classroom door ordering the students to finish a worksheet that she had given them. The students basically ignored her requests. When I arrived, one of the students, Camilla, told me that they weren't going in because that teacher "didn't know how to teach," and just kept wasting their time. Camilla complained that she and other students wanted to learn, but that the teacher wasn't teaching math, but just kept giving them the same kind of low-level worksheet. They felt she couldn't answer their questions and apparently didn't know the subject. Camilla and others announced that they were not planning to go back into the classroom until they had a new teacher.

Again, it would have been easy to threaten them, to start calling parents, to suspend or expel the leaders like Camilla. Because they knew and liked me, I might have even been successful at ordering them back into the classroom. Instead, after we talked a little about their concerns (with which I agreed, although I didn't let them know), I asked them each to write down their specific concerns. I told them I would take their written concerns to the principal and discuss them with her, but that if the concerns weren't written, they would lack validity and could not be brought to her attention. After completing their letters of complaint, we talked about the worksheet. While Camilla was still insisting they wouldn't do it, I asked her to consider how the other adults in the school might interpret their behavior. I suggested that if they saw students refusing to work, they might feel much more inclined to sympathize with the teacher. On the other hand, if they all did their work, other adults would say, "Look at these students. They really want to work, so there must be something to their concerns about the teacher." Eventually, Camilla and a few others agreed and directed the class to work on the worksheet. I took Camilla aside and told her that the other thing that might hurt their cause was the few students who were fooling around, roaming the halls of the school. Camilla then took it upon herself to round up the wayward students and sit them down for a lecture on how they were supposed to act if they really wanted change to happen; they were not going to get rid of that teacher if they acted goofy and weren't serious. She was an impressive presenter!

The teacher was indeed replaced, with the stipulation that it was now the students' job to make sure the new teacher, who definitely knew math and wanted them to be successful, would have their full cooperation. The students went back to class, Camilla learned some of the rules and responsibilities of leadership, and I learned that listening to the students and reasoning with them went much further than strong-arming them into compliance. The class ended the year successfully.

There are many other stories to tell about my year in this school of sixth to tenth graders, stories that challenged the adults to think fast, to care, and to listen.

Sometimes we did and sometimes our adult behavior left much to be desired. I tell these stories because reading this book brought them and many others vividly to mind. If I had had this book that year, I wonder if I could have had more productive conversations with the teachers, parents, administrators, and even the students themselves. On one hand, I see the book as providing an opportunity for aspiring and new teachers to gain insight into teaching from the people most affected by their success or failure. On the other, I see it also as a catalyst for experienced teachers to rethink their craft and to use the words of the students in the book to initiate conversations with their own students.

The words of the students in this book ring true. As a "mother" of a school who had the luxury of talking and listening to students on a daily basis, without having the daily responsibility of teaching, I can attest to the accuracy with which Kathleen Cushman has captured her student co-authors' voices. I can only hope that those who have not yet learned to hear the voices of their own students will be inspired to ask and listen. For my money, there is no better teacher education.

CHAPTER 1

Knowing Students Well

"IF YOU PAY ATTENTION, YOU CAN SEE IT."

By the time they reach their teens, students have a high stake in how they want others to see them—not only their peers, but also their teachers.

> We want a balance. Every student wants to feel special and smart and talented, but at the same time we want to blend in. VANCE

They want teachers to understand the obstacles they face in their everyday lives. But they vary considerably, like adults, in how much of their personal lives they are willing to share with others—especially those who wield power over them.

> Get to know their neighborhood—see if students are having a hard time. PORSCHE

> I don't want a teacher knowing too much about me. Don't be singing Happy Birthday when I come in to class. BOSUNG

They recognize condescension immediately. When it comes from an imbalance of power—whether deriving from age, ethnicity, class, gender, or language— their responses range from defiance to embarrassment.

> It doesn't work when a teacher tries to force the connection or try too hard to relate to us. When they say, "I understand what you're going through," we know they don't. TIFFANY

> Some teachers pretend to understand because of what they saw in a movie or read in a book. Or they corner a student to find out more about

them, like "How does it feel to be black?" It's pretty obvious that the only reason they're talking to you is to try to find out information. Just let things come up casually, don't pull a student out of class. DARYL

WHAT SHOULD A TEACHER KNOW ABOUT STUDENTS?

Students want teachers to know their strengths and acknowledge their expertise, but they rarely get a chance to make them known. Eight of this book's co-authors—newcomers to this country who are still learning English—made the following list of what they already know and can do:

I know Latin dance, from Peru. RAFAEL

I can play the organ. LUCIANA

I play guitar. I want to join a band. JAE YOON

I have a black belt in judo. I learned in Japan, when I was a little girl. TSUGUMI

I know how to swim and play piano, but I stopped when I came here from Hong Kong because I don't have time. KAREN

I can draw the Aztec calendar. And I fix things like lights, and chairs. My uncle taught me when I came from Mexico. PEDRO

I write poems. And I like to paint flowers and people. But the brush and paints cost $65! ELAINE

I know soccer. I learned it in Mexico. And I know how to make organic pasta from my restaurant job here. JAVIER

Co-authors whose English was more proficient wrote longer lists. Bosung is good at card tricks, and has created a four-minute Korean rap music video at his Korean-language school. Daryl has an interest in the Bible and mythology. Tiffany has researched sexually transmitted diseases and works as a peer counselor in a community youth-action group. Maribel's mother sometimes takes her to work and encourages her to speak in public. Many of these students play sports, dance, sing, or play an instrument.

Though their teachers know little about these interests and talents, the students themselves are aware they have real meaning.

> I like to go on the Internet and look for Japanese cartoons. You can learn a lot from cartoons. One of them was about revolts—the government was corrupt, and one character said: "History is like an endless waltz, it never ends, it keeps going on and on." MARIBEL

They recognize the learning opportunities their skills provide.

> Sometimes we know what other people don't know, and we can explain to them. JAVIER

> My first English teacher in middle school saw me and my friend dancing, and she made a class after school for us to teach samba to English-speaking kids. Teachers can make connections for us if they know what we can do. ELAINE

HOW CAN A TEACHER LEARN ABOUT STUDENTS?

Getting to know students doesn't happen all at once. It builds over time, through paying attention to what individual students say and do—and what they don't—in the classroom and hallways, in their written work, speech patterns, and physical appearance. A group of student co-authors talked about the signals to watch for:

> Don't just look at students for answers, but look at who we *are*, through the way we act. Not "what's going on in our home life"—be perceptive to what's going on in our *classroom*. Who we like, what's hard for us, what's easy for us. If you pay attention, you can see it.
>
> Don't be afraid to talk to us one on one, but don't try too hard to be our friend.
>
> We don't want something so obvious. We want you to notice the little signals we give in class—the way we answer a question, if we stutter a little or we pause—
>
> Even the way we look at you! Our body language—
>
> If there's confusion on my face, I want you to see it. If there's disagreement, I want you to say, "You disagree? Why?"
>
> And without talking to a student for eighteen hours, know them well enough to know what their faces mean.

They offered a variety of techniques for teachers to use in getting to know their students:

Questionnaires. Teachers can learn much of what they need to know about students simply by asking them. Giving out a questionnaire on the first day of a new class shows students that the teacher cares about their strengths, interests, backgrounds, and concerns about the subject area of the class.

Knowing all these things early on helps you to know them as a person. It gives you a sense of how to reach them, what they think is funny, that kind of thing. It can help a teacher to watch out for warning signs in discussions. VANCE

If you ask the student questions right away, you eliminate the strangeness early. So if a student needs to go to you for help, they won't feel so weird or strange. Or if you ask someone to present in front of the class and you know they have had a bad experience with that in the past, it might explain why they say No. Or if they're religious, they might not want to cut a pig, they might have holidays you don't know about. MIKA

In history the first day my teacher passed out a paper with a couple of questions about how you learn—like: what type of issues do you have with history, do you like it? That was the first time a teacher seemed to actually care about how a student learns, so she could meet their needs. It made me think about how I learn—I never thought about it before, because I'd never been asked. TIFFANY

Questions should invite responses on a range of topics, but teachers should make clear that students don't need to respond to questions they don't feel comfortable answering. Boys and girls may have different tolerance levels, and cultural norms about privacy may be a factor as well.

Nothing personal! Guidance counselors are for students' personal help. Teachers are for teaching. BOSUNG

On pages 9 to 11, a sample questionnaire (easily adapted to various teachers' situations) combines suggestions from all the student co-authors.

Get to know their neighborhoods. Nothing opens a teacher's eyes more to the lives of students than taking the time to see where they live. Especially if commuting to a teaching job from another neighborhood, teachers may not be aware of the context in which students spend their lives outside of school. Can they count on reliable public transportation, a convenient public library, a clean and safe environment? These factors—and many more that teachers can see if they keep their eyes open—affect students' ability to do well in school.

At one San Francisco Bay Area high school, student leaders started up "teacher tours," in which small groups of students signed up to take teachers on car tours of their neighborhoods. With one teacher at the wheel and another in the passenger seat, students point out such landmarks as where they go to church, where a younger brother goes to day care or a parent works, where they pass a drug dealers' gathering spot on their way home.

Students want teachers to know these things, but they also are sensitive to the assumptions adults may make based on their neighborhood.

> When you talk about your neighborhood, it's a more open way to approach learning personal things. But it's easy to assume things about a student based on their neighborhood or their race and class—like if you're black, "You like basketball, huh?" They say, "You don't talk like someone from Harlem." We don't have to be reminded by you of what the stereotypes are.
> VANCE

> Just because I live in Harlem doesn't mean my brother sells drugs, I live in a crack-abandoned building, or I'm on welfare. Someone I know comes to my apartment and says, "Wow, I didn't know you lived in a place like this," because the house is clean. ALEXIS

If they see drug dealers, they'll think that's why you're so dumb. My street is so nasty, and it's hard to walk by. You can see the needles. VERONICA

People don't want to come to my neighborhood because they're afraid of it. Our apartment is beautiful and spotless, there are mirrors all around and it's kind of like a house. But the outside of it is just horrible, so my mom doesn't like to invite people over. LAURALIZ

And though students understand the importance of communicating with parents, they definitely do not want teachers visiting their homes.

No going to the home. Teenagers don't think of themselves as children, even from the ninth grade. Teachers should realize that they're working with kids who feel that they are somewhat adults and don't like to be treated as little kids. ALEXIS

A new teacher should always talk to a parent and let them know what the kids should be doing in that year. And they can call them if they don't come to the conferences, if they're supposed to. But I would not like it myself if the teacher came to my home. They've seen my house and they know everything. That would be uncomfortable for me. LAURALIZ

Have students keep a journal. Whether the subject is literature or history or math, making time in class for students to keep a journal can offer a teacher an invaluable look at who their students are. Even ten minutes of writing a week will help, using prompts such as "What's going on with you that affects your learning in this class?" or "What should I know about how you are doing in this class this week?" Teachers may find out something about their own teaching, or about their students' other commitments:

In my chemistry class the teacher just keeps going and going and writing on the board. She never stops to ask the class, "Is everyone with me?" She's in her own little world. She never turns around, she just talks to the board, not to us. TIFFANY

Some teachers don't have any idea what you do, and they give you three hours of homework. If they get an idea, then it would be more healthy and give us better learning opportunities. We might actually learn something instead of trying to cram everything into one night. BOSUNG

Collect and read the journals, and write some response in it, however short. Even something like "I didn't know that!" or "Thank you" will keep the information coming and make the student feel more connected. Stay away from judgmental comments, and don't grade the journal. It's a place for acceptance, reflection, and connection.

Finally, unless students are writing about doing harm to themselves or others, they need to know that teachers will keep the information they share confidential. They don't want to hear things about themselves coming back to them from a third party.

WHO ARE YOU? A Questionnaire for Students on the First Day of School

Note: I will not share your answers with anyone without your permission.

Basic information:

Name:_____

Name you like to be called: _____

Date of birth:_____ Place of birth: _____

Email address: _____ Phone number: _____

Parents' or guardians' names: _____

Any siblings? What ages? Do they live with you?_____

_____

Others who live in your household? _____

_____

Who would you like me to tell when you do something especially well? _____

_____

What language do you speak at home? _____

Are you new to this school? Where were you before? _____

_____

About your activities and interests:

What time do you usually get up in the morning?_____

How do you get to school?_____ How long does it take? _____

What do you do after school?_____

_____

When do you usually go to bed at night? _____

What are your other interests?_____

_____

What do you imagine yourself doing ten years from now? _____

_____

About the way you learn:

Do you like this subject? Why or why not? _____

_____

What would you really like to learn about in this class? _____

_____

What's a fair amount of homework time to expect you to give to this class?

_____

Describe the way you learn things best._____

_____

How do you feel about working in groups?_____

_____

Is there anything that could make this class especially hard for you?_____

_____

Can you think of a way I could help you with this? _____

_____

Is there anything else about you that you would like me to know?

_____

_____

_____

_____

_____

It's okay to share information—it can help you if it's done in a respectful way. But sometimes teachers tell you that they are talking about you in the teachers' lounge. If you're going to do that, you should tell the student directly, so it doesn't come back to you from another teacher, like they're talking behind your back. VERONICA

Ask students about their schedules. Teachers need to know what commitments students face on a daily basis outside school. Are students working after school, perhaps to help support their families? Do they play sports, have church activities, do housework, make dinner, or take care of younger siblings? Take ten minutes out of a class to ask students to write down what they do in a typical day, from the time they wake up to when they go to sleep. Here is one such list from Porsche, an Oakland student:

6:30 A.M.	Wake up
7:00 A.M.	Wash up and get dressed
8:00 A.M.	Walk my sisters (ages 6 and 7) to school
8:25 A.M.–3:25 P.M.	Go to school
3:25–3:50 P.M.	Catch the bus to practice
4:00–6:00 P.M.	Badminton practice
6:00–7:30 P.M.	Go to Merritt College to run on the track for school team
7:30–8:00 P.M.	Catch the bus home
8:00–8:30 P.M.	Do the chores, clean the kitchen, help my little brother and two sisters do their homework
8:30–9:30 P.M.	Do my homework
9:30–10:45 P.M.	Watch TV
10:45–11:59 P.M.	Talk on the telephone
12:00 A.M.–6:30 A.M.	Take my medicine and go to sleep

None of her teachers knows her after-school schedule, Porsche said.

> I don't care if they know, because it probably wouldn't make a difference for some of them. They would probably make me quit playing sports, if it's up to them.

But if they knew what she did each day, her teachers would at least have a much better picture of who Porsche is, what motivates her, and what they might realistically expect her to complete for homework. How many people, after a full day of work and more than three hours of exercise, are ready for intellectual activity at 8:30 P.M.?

Connect academic work to students' interests. If teachers know more about what their students care about, it's easier to motivate them, by connecting academic work to their existing interests.

> I think one of the only ways people learn something alien is to relate it to their own experience. If a teacher can connect geometry and angles to my interest in art or being an actor, that works. Even though I know I didn't grow up with math, I know enough because he relates it to me. VANCE

> My global teacher turns it into personal experience so you can relate to the way you feel. Maybe his grandfather fought in the Vietnam War, so then I get interested in what happened in that war, who was the president, stuff like that. It makes you think: maybe I can relate it to my life. LAURALIZ

> In chemistry we were learning about bonds: chemical bonds, carbon bonds—and she related it to dating! It was good—she would say: "A covalent bond is like not actually having a boyfriend but dating two different people." TIFFANY

I used to hate to read a lot, but when we were reading about Malcolm X in my American lit class, that was important to me. MAHOGANY

If there was a school where teachers would ask me every day things that I would be interested in, I would have a different feeling about school. But you can't do that because you have your subjects and you can't make them into things I would be interested in. For example, I would take no math at all, no history, no subjects that you have in school besides science. I might like school if it was about animals, because I want to be a vet or work with animals. I would do the other work for that, though I would probably look for something that did not involve math. DIANA

Students know that school can help them develop their interests and passions, but often their teachers don't have enough information to help that happen— particularly if language forms a barrier. But it's worth the trouble to find out. For example, eleven co-authors who are English-language learners made a chart describing how their teachers could help them realize their long-term dreams. In almost every case, they laid out short-term goals that involved improving their English and doing challenging work that would support their interests. (See Chapter 8, page 161.)

DON'T BE A STRANGER

Finally, though adolescents often hide it, they are interested in their teachers' lives, too. This doesn't mean that teachers need to reveal personal information, but students welcome anything teachers are willing to share about their academic training, work background, or outside interests. Student co-authors listed the following questions they'd like to ask their teachers:

WHAT WE'D LIKE TO KNOW ABOUT YOU

Where did you go to college?

Did you have other jobs before this one? What were they?

Why did you become a teacher? Why this subject?

Are you married? Do you have any kids?

Answering honestly can help win students' trust.

Summary

GETTING TO KNOW US

Do . . .	Don't . . .
Give us a questionnaire on the first day of class, asking about our strengths, interests, backgrounds, and concerns. (See pages 9–11 for a sample questionnaire.)	Ask us to share information we consider private.
Get to know our neighborhoods. (See pages 6–7 for an example of how to do this.)	Make assumptions about us based on where we live.
	Visit our homes without our knowledge or permission.
Have us keep a journal (of our responses to readings, question prompts, or whatever we choose). Read and respond to our entries regularly.	Share information about us from questionnaires or journals without our permission (unless we plan to harm ourselves or others).
Find out what our daily schedule includes (other classes, sports, job, family obligations).	Judge or grade the contents of our journals.
Assign academic work that connects to our interests, and invite us to use our existing knowledge and experience in carrying it out.	

CHAPTER 2

Respect, Liking, Trust, and Fairness

"IF YOU SEE THE TEACHER RESPECT STUDENTS, YOU'LL FOLLOW THAT ROLE MODEL."

In the high school classroom, respect and trust travel a two-way street between teacher and student—and have everything to do with learning. Students say that if a teacher sets a steady example of fairness and respect, they respond positively whether or not they like a teacher personally. If they trust a teacher to do the job with competence and without bias, they are willing to fulfill their part of the deal: to pay attention, do the work, and play by the rules.

> There was this guy who coached track. If he told you to do twenty laps and the guys were complaining, he would say: "Okay, do five." If you were tired, he would say, "Okay, you can stop." He would take you out for pizza after practice. He was a cool coach; they all loved him. But when the time for the meets came, they never won anything. So they got a new coach. The new coach, if he says, "Do fifty laps," and they say, "We don't wanna," he'll say, "Oh, no? Then do fifty-two!" They hated him because he made them work so hard. But when the time for the meets came, they won every single time. They learned the difference between respecting and liking. ALEXIS

> Being able to trust your teacher and be trusted is important. One student in my school was homeless. The principal wasn't like, "Let's go to your house and talk to your mom." He was like, "If you need a safe place to stay, I know someone you can talk to." He doesn't want you to feel embarrassed. When they have teacher conferences, he does not tell other people private things you have told him. If you're gay, if you're

getting beat up, if you're not eating, if you're dealing with identity problems, you can tell him! Because you *know* that it is affecting your work.
You can talk about it with him, and he'll keep giving you chances, even
if you keep messing up. If going to homework lab after school doesn't
work, he'll try something else. ALEXIS

How can new high school teachers, who sometimes look and feel quite close to
their students in age, strike that balance of respect, trust, and fairness? How
does mutual respect in high school show itself—and what, if anything, does it
have to do with how much a student and teacher like each other? What builds
trust between teachers and students, and what breaks it down? At a time when
students are just developing into adults, how much leeway do they need to
make mistakes?

I'm not adult enough to get a job and have my own apartment, but I'm
adult enough to make decisions on my own, know right from wrong,
have ideas about the world. That's why it's hard to be a teenager—it's
like a middle stage. VANCE

If I have to go to the bathroom, and you tell me not to go, I'm going to
go anyway. I'm not trying to be disrespectful, but certain teachers ask
me to do something that compromises myself, and I'll say no. It has its
effects—then you don't call on me, or you have an expression on your
face. You're attacking me back in class. You shouldn't show that it bothers
you. It shouldn't have to show in front of other students. Don't ignore
me. I'm a student. Yeah, I should have respected you, but you're thirty
or forty years old, an adult—you should rise above it, not continue the
animosity. No teacher should be rolling their eyes at me. ALEXIS

One group of student co-authors made up the following rules of thumb they thought applied equally to teachers and students:

IF YOU'RE LOOKING FOR RESPECT . . .

Show up on time.

Take your responsibility seriously, whatever it is. Do what you agreed to do.

Don't insult people's intelligence.

Respect others' right to a separate identity, even if it's not the one you choose.

Don't assume you know everything about someone.

Be careful what you say. Don't make jokes until you know people well enough.

DO STUDENTS NEED TO LIKE A TEACHER?

Everyone likes some people better than others, including students and teachers. But in general kids want teachers to put good teaching ahead of popularity.

It's okay if kids hate you at first. If you care about your teaching, we'll get past that. We're not going to be receptive to someone so quickly—we're kind of young in our thinking. MIKA

To a certain extent you have to have a personality that students respond to. But that doesn't mean you have to be our best friend, because that will cause our education to suffer. I hate to admit it, but respect and authority are part of the job. Kids expect adults to give us directions and boundaries, but it's a balance. VANCE

Students often like a teacher who has something in common with them, who seems approachable, or who is closer to their generation and more familiar with youth culture. Though they don't need to know a lot about a teacher's private life, they appreciate a degree of openness and humor.

> I relate to one teacher well and a lot of people don't. She is somewhat like me (very sarcastic and moody at times), and I think that's why we click. We talk like we're buddies, and she's always encouraging me. ALEXIS

> The teacher should fill out the same questionnaire and share his answers with the students. Let them laugh at him a little. There's nothing like laughing at a teacher. LAURALIZ

Liking a teacher can help with learning.

> It kind of ruins a subject if you don't like the teacher. I never liked history at all. But this year I have a really cool teacher, and so even if it's hard, even if I don't do well on tests, I'm starting to like it more. BOSUNG

> I really hate calculus, but I really like the teacher so I really work hard and do my homework. TIFFANY

> I have to somewhat like the teacher to be able to learn—to know I can go to that person and ask for help when I need it, and he will be okay with it. LAURALIZ

But most students are also ready to learn from teachers they may not like on a personal level. Whether or not they like them, they gain more from teachers who care about their material and commit themselves to students' learning.

I don't have to act like I like you, and you don't have to act like you like me, in order for me to learn and you to teach. [I don't like] the way my math teacher teaches, but I know that the way he comes into a classroom, he wants the students to leave knowing math. This makes me open my mind to what he has to say and how he's trying to say it. I'm going to learn whether or not the teacher and I are friends. As long as a teacher is real and the student is real and they are acting in a respectful way, there can be a give-and-take relationship with information. MIKA

I liked my Spanish teacher most. She was a good teacher but she would get off the subject and talk about other things—she was very easily distracted. She was funny and I like funny teachers. But I learned more from my global studies teacher. He is a great teacher—very serious and strict. He really cares about students; you can tell he likes to teach. He sticks to the subject. It wasn't easy to distract him. When he's done with the lesson he'll make one joke and that will be it—and it will relate to the subject. LAURALIZ

MUST TEACHERS LIKE STUDENTS?

It matters to students that teachers like being in their company.

It's not as important for a teacher to like the students as it is for the students to think the teacher likes them. Students feel more comfortable and motivated in classes where they think the teacher likes them. DARYL

But when teachers appear to like some students more than others, they feel uncomfortable, whether or not they count among the favored.

I would rather not know if I'm a teacher's favorite. It puts me in a weird position. When we're having a test or something, other students will come up to me and say, "Why don't you ask if we can not have it—she likes you." TIFFANY

My French teacher has a very disturbing habit of calling some of his students his "advanced" students. This gives those that are not "advanced" a feeling of lesser value, and feelings of anger come up. He creates a barrier between himself and students, and even between students in the class. BOSUNG

If teachers don't like students, the students can also tell, and it affects their learning. Even the suspicion that a teacher holds a bias sometimes grows into students feeling that they can't do anything right.

If the teacher doesn't like you, they won't say, "You can do it," or push you to your full potential. If you miss a day at school, they won't say what you missed and help you out. MONTOYA

My friend said one little thing, and now that's the end of her. The teacher wrote her off, so she has a 65 now and I have a 90 and we have done nothing different. LAURALIZ

Most students would rather stay somewhere in the middle, not singled out for favor or disfavor. They may not feel comfortable making a personal connection until after a course has ended.

When I'm their student, I go to them for help and nothing else —it's just something I have. After I'm not their student anymore, I might go to them just to talk; I tell them how my new teacher is, and how I like my new class. MARIBEL

THE IMPORTANCE OF SELF-RESPECT

Students respect teachers who are comfortable with themselves. Even when teachers come from a different background than students do, if they convey self-respect, kids will respond.

> A student has enough common sense to see something in the teacher that they connect with. The teacher doesn't have to throw it to them— the student will choose to make the connection because they see it.
> ALEXIS

> The teacher has to not be afraid to show himself, and at the same time maintain a boundary. Don't try to look like me, talk like me, dress like me, put your hair in cornrows. The minute you try to broadcast about yourself in order to make a connection with the kid, that's the minute it fails, because we can sniff out that kind of thing. If you just keep teaching, you will eventually reach someone. We'll put in the effort to connect with you. VANCE

And they want teachers to act like adults, confident and authoritative.

> If you start as an authority figure, the relationships will come. You can get friendly later on. And you can be friendly and still be strict. You have to let them know that you're not one of their peers. BOSUNG

> If you are too friendly with the students, when things get out of control and you try to get authoritative, they're like, "yeah, whatever," and don't pay any attention. TIFFANY

FAIRNESS BUILDS TRUST AND RESPECT

Students know that by coming to school they are making a bargain with teachers,[*] and they want it to be a fair one. Here's how they define it:

THE BARGAIN WE MAKE WITH TEACHERS

If you will . . .	Then we will . . .
Show you know and care about the material	Believe the material can be important for us to learn
Treat us as smart and capable of challenging work	Feel respected and rise to the challenge of demanding work
Allow us increasing independence but agree with us on clear expectations	Learn to act responsibly on our own, though we will sometimes make mistakes in the process
Model how to act when you or we make mistakes	Learn to take intellectual risks; learn to make amends when we behave badly
Show respect for our differences and individual styles	Let you limit some of our freedoms in the interest of the group
Keep private anything personal we tell you	Trust you with information that could help you teach us better

Whether they are "hard" or "easy" teachers, the adults who win students' trust and respect are the ones perceived as scrupulously fair in carrying out this usually unspoken bargain. From the very first day, students are alert to signals of whether the teacher will uphold it—and that will largely determine whether they in turn will do their part. Our students listed the following things they hope their teachers will do:

---

[*] We are grateful to Joseph McDonald at New York University for his framing of "the deal" between students and teachers in a work in progress he shared with us. It afforded an invaluable construct through which our student co-authors explored and analyzed their experiences.

Let us know what to expect from you and the class. When you ask us about ourselves on the first day (see pages 9–11), answer our questions, too. You don't have to reveal anything you consider private (like whether you have a girlfriend or boyfriend), but we should know certain things from the start. Do you give a zero when homework is not turned in on time? Do you count class participation as part of the final grade?

SOME THINGS WE WANT TO KNOW ON THE FIRST DAY

What will we be studying or doing during this course?

What can we expect for pop quizzes, tests, essays, or projects?

Do you give a lot of homework?

What is your grading system?

Is this class going to be fun? If not, what will make it interesting?

Will you be available to help us outside class?

Know your material.

It feels like we're being punished when the teacher doesn't know the subject well enough to help students. The student has to move on the next year to a higher level, and they'll be stumped in the next year. It's kind of not fair. ANDRES

I had a math and chemistry teacher that didn't know either subject. If you were quiet, you got an A, and if you were talking, you wouldn't do well. It kind of makes me angry in a way, because when you get to college you'll be stuck. It's okay for a teacher to learn, but they shouldn't take your time to learn it. MAHOGANY

Push us to do our best—

I had a math teacher who was always on your case: "Write out the problem, turn in your work, you can do it." I didn't like the way he pushed me. But later I thought he was a good teacher—the little things, like "make sure you don't forget to write it all out"—those are the things you need to remember. DIANA

My algebra teacher, when I got a C in his class, he was upset. He just pushed me to keep my head outa them boys and into the books. He made me go to tutoring after school to keep my grades up. PORSCHE

—and push us equally.

I have a teacher who pushes the "good" students a lot more than the not-so-good students. Like when a straight-A student doesn't do the work, he'll give that person lectures, but when a lower-grade student doesn't do the work, he'll just give up, like he didn't expect it anyway. DIANA

Some teachers give more of themselves to students who succeed rather than fail. It feels like they're saying, "You're not worth my time because I'm dealing with students who have more potential than you." I don't feel that "go-go-go!" from them. ALEXIS

Do your part.

You have teachers that are not even responsible. They're not even in class—they leave you there. They give you the assignment and just walk around the halls. PORSCHE

One teacher made us redo an assignment that I was sure that I had already done, then claimed that we had done it all wrong, just to cover up for the fact that he had lost the assignments. It was an insult to my pride, a waste of time, and a blatant lie. "Because I said so," or "Because I am the teacher," are also not good explanations for punishments. Teachers must be clear and fair, or students will be hurt or angry. BOSUNG

Make sure everyone understands. Give the slower students among us a chance without putting them on the spot.

When you have a question, it's better if the teacher comes and stands by your desk instead of saying "What do you need?" from across the room. PORSCHE

[Some teachers] don't care whether you're smart or dumb. They don't talk to you; if you're failing a class they don't ask you "What's the matter?" They let you fail, and they don't give you makeup work. MONTOYA

Grade us fairly.

If someone gives you a bad grade, they should tell you exactly why. We have this Spanish teacher that grades Latino kids so hard it's impossible for them to get As no matter how hard you try. DIANA

Sometimes [favoritism] shows in their opinions on papers and comments on grades—which is the worst thing, because students always compare their grades with each other. MARIBEL

AM I PLAYING FAVORITES? A Reflective Exercise for Teachers

Pick out a representative mix of students from your class. Using copies of this questionnaire or blank pages in a notebook or journal, answer the following questions.

Student's name _____

Things I like about the student

Personal choices (clothes, hair, posture, language, cooperation)

_____

_____

Academic choices (does work, participates)

_____

_____

Things that annoy me about the student

Personal choices (clothes, hair, posture, language, rule-breaking)

_____

_____

Academic choices (does work, participates)

_____

_____

Positive attention I paid the student today *(check any that apply)*

☐ Called on in an encouraging way

☐ Asked how things are going

☐ Trusted with an important responsibility

☐ Asked his or her thoughts on a question that matters

☐ Acknowledged good work or helpful contribution by student

☐ Responded to something in the student's writing

Negative attention I paid the student today

☐ Used sarcasm in class to make my point with the student

☐ Criticized in class

☐ Did not offer specific encouragement to speak

☐ Imposed behavior sanctions (gave detention, sent to office, etc.)

Most recent grade(s) I gave the student _____

After you have completed the questionnaire for several students, look over the results and reflect in writing on the following questions:

Did students with lower grades have more "personal choices" that annoyed me?

Did students with higher grades receive more positive attention from me?

What could I do to increase positive attention to students whose choices annoy me?

Understand that we make mistakes.

> Because of something that happened in ninth grade, she won't sit down with me and talk to me about anything. So I do the same back to her— I don't smile at her or respect her. Teachers need to make allowance for the fact that we change from year to year and even from week to week. Sometimes I'm just acting hotheaded, I need to clear the air and then come back and apologize. I can acknowledge the things I do wrong.
> ALEXIS

> We're some moody-ass people right now! MIKA

> We're growing. VANCE

Don't denigrate us, especially in public.

> One teacher would say out loud, "You're getting a D," or other negative things in front of other students, disrespecting them. MAHOGANY

> I respect this one teacher, but I feel like she doesn't respect me. She'll say things in front of the class that make me feel bad, like "you didn't do this" or "you did this wrong." DIANA

Keep your biases to yourself.

> This gay kid in my class was putting something on his lips, and the teacher said, "You don't need to put on lip gloss in class!" If a girl put on lip gloss in class, he wouldn't say that. Then the boys in class felt like they could laugh at that kid. If the teacher could make comments, they felt like they could, too. TIFFANY

By the looks of a kid, some teachers think he'll be a troublemaker. People say, "They're black, they do drugs," that kind of thing. If the teacher judges kids like that, the kids start saying the teacher's racist and they have less respect for that teacher. MARIBEL

Don't treat us like little kids.

Teenagers don't think of themselves as children, even from the ninth grade. Teachers should realize that they're working with kids who feel that they are somewhat adults and don't like to be treated as little kids, even though in actuality they are kids. In my mind you're not my parent, you're my teacher. That line goes but so far. Don't overstep your boundary. ALEXIS

Part of a teacher's job is giving teenagers the practice at that independence—not just controlling the kids in their classes but actually giving them more ability to try things out for themselves. MAHOGANY

Listen to what we think.

Some teachers have a way of making themselves more approachable. They do not seem like hard, old teachers who sternly instruct the class; a student can go up and carry out a conversation without feeling awkward. This gives the class a more comfortable and accepting atmosphere to learn in. BOSUNG

Sometimes my teachers ask me things like, "What grade do you think I'm going to give you if you didn't do the work?" Then they get upset if I seem to actually be thinking of what the answer might be. A lot of times I'm not interested in the work. DIANA

QUESTIONS WE WISH A TEACHER WOULD ASK

Would you like extra credit?

Will you be able to do homework over the weekend?

How would you like to make up your homework/projects?

How are you feeling—do you want to do your work right now, or for homework?

Do you need a ride to and from school?

Do you have lunch money?

What could I be doing to help you learn better?

Care what's going on with us.

Some teachers start to fill a void that maybe isn't being addressed at home. Teachers are our de facto parents for the seven or so hours you're with them. I don't really have a father, so I guess it's important talking to a guy who seems to know what's going on in the world, respects you, knows what's going on with you. VANCE

School lets you find some adults you can connect with. There might be something really important, like pregnancy, that you can't talk to your parents about, but you know you have to talk to adults about. I have one of these relationships with my adviser. I think I trust him because I see him so often; he's my teacher for two classes, and I have a free [period] with him. ANDRES

Don't betray our confidences.

> You want to be able to trust a teacher. You don't want to be telling them your problem and then have them go to other teachers and say you have a problem, or tell your mom you should see a psychiatrist. Some teachers, it's like you tell them something and then there's a microphone attached to them. PORSCHE

> If you have that trust with a teacher, it could go kind of wrong. They might look down on you because you did something that you're not telling other people. It makes you wonder if it will affect how you do in their class. ANDRES

Sometimes the chance to stand in each other's shoes can build respect between teachers and students.

> In the very beginning of the class, our teacher had us write for homework one night about how we would teach a history class if we were teachers. She didn't use what I wrote down, but it got the students to recognize how hard it was to teach it. HILARY

> One day we had to plan a lesson. She gave us a topic, and we had to research it and make a lesson plan. Each day the students got to teach, and we got to see where she was coming from, in terms of having everyone in the class pay attention and learn from you. That changed our class a lot—now every time we get disruptive, she reminds us how we felt in that situation. MAHOGANY

FAIRNESS AFFECTS CLASSROOM BEHAVIOR

A teacher's fairness, trust, and respect have a lot of influence on how students feel about themselves and about their teachers. But they also have an important effect on students' behavior in the classroom.

> The worst thing for a teacher is to be considered unfair, because students then try to take advantage of it. If you're the favorite one, you think you can get away with certain things. If you're the "down" one, sometimes you can shut yourself off, or try to control the class instead of the teacher. MARIBEL

> If you hurt me with your words, I'm gonna say or do something that I know is gonna hurt you. ALEXIS

In the next chapter, we will explore the ways that a teacher can use fairness, trust, and respect to achieve a classroom where students' behavior is an asset, not a problem.

Summary

HOW TO SHOW RESPECT, TRUST, AND FAIRNESS

- Let us know what to expect from you and from the class.

- Know your material.

- Push us to do our best—and push us equally.

- Do your part.

- Make sure everyone understands.

- Grade us fairly.

- Understand that we make mistakes.

- Don't denigrate us.

- Keep your biases to yourself.

- Don't treat us like little kids.

- Listen to what we think.

- Care what's going on with us.

- Don't betray our confidences.

CHAPTER 3

Classroom Behavior

"A LOT OF PEOPLE ARE AFRAID OF TEENAGERS. THEY THINK WE ARE THESE FREAK
HUMANS."

An orderly, purposeful classroom matters just as much to kids as it does to teachers.

> It doesn't feel so good when I'm in this class where half the kids are taking over, jumping, screaming, taking over the conversation, not letting the teacher talk. The other half just zone out—some sleep, some do other work. Some complain: "Why am I here? This class makes no sense."
> MARIBEL

> When I be in a class like that, I feel like the kids are wasting my time, because I want to learn. MONTOYA

But in a disruptive classroom, a host of coded signs are circulating, messages students want their teachers to understand:

> If a teacher's done something wrong but doesn't believe it's wrong, I want to give him trouble, to try to change his view. DARYL

> If a teacher shows that they're scared of the students, the students are going to try to take control. VERONICA

A teacher who wants a classroom that works has to fulfill the bargain students described in Chapter 2: Know and care about the material, treat kids with respect and fairness, and they will pay attention, do the work, give up some freedom, and play by the rules. Students realize that this bargain will pay off eventually, in learning and life success. But if teachers signal unwillingness to keep up their part, kids will immediately act to right the balance of power that makes the deal fair. The struggle that results is what many people consider an "out of control classroom."

This chapter includes many examples of unacceptable classroom behavior—by both students and teachers. It aims not to scare or depress, but to offer practice in seeing the bargain from both sides. If teachers can get used to doing that, their interactions with students will take place on a clear and straightforward basis. Their actions and words will have consequences, and so will their students'—a fair deal to remind them of whenever necessary.

STARTING OUT ON THE RIGHT FOOT

From the first class meeting, students will be looking for signs that a teacher is willing to do his or her part in helping them get what they need from school. Chapters 1 and 2 offer many practical ways to convey answers to students' two central questions:

> Are you genuinely interested in who we are and what we already know?

> Do you treat us with respect, in both personal and academic matters?

But other important signals—about what teachers expect from students in the way of classroom behavior—will also come across in what a teacher says and does from the start. Students expect the following:

Let students know your plan for the class.

> Put an agenda on the board. DIANA

> Even if it's really basic, like: "Problems. Discussion." Then at least you know they have something planned. Otherwise sometimes it's clear that they don't know what they are going to do. HILARY

> If a teacher comes in and is not prepared, you have no other choice but start talking to your neighbor. So it's really important to come prepared. At least have a warm-up for kids to do while you get your things together. MAHOGANY

Discuss expectations for classroom behavior. Students understand that different teachers need different things in order to maintain a good learning environment. Teachers should say what they need with regard to food and drink, speaking out, language, lateness, homework completion, attentiveness, classroom housekeeping, and other behavior that helps reach, or detracts from, the goals of the class. Invite students to add their own needs to the list, and come to agreement on conflicts. Teachers should also make clear when they plan to assess classroom behavior and work habits as part of the grade. (The same goes when planning some other reward or punishment for behavior, such as participation in a field trip, or detention.) Finally, put your policies on all these things in writing, either for handing out to students or posting on the classroom walls.

> My new teacher didn't set boundaries about what was okay to do. Kids would take out sports or motorcycle magazines in the middle of a class discussion—the first time it happened, he should have addressed it right away. Instead he waited a couple of days. DARYL

> Students don't want only the principals and teachers to be in control, they want the students to be more involved. ANDRES

Find out what the school expects in terms of formal policies and more informal practices.

> Be observant of how things are done in the school—what its policies are on chewing gum, homework, grades, language in the classroom, clothes. MIKA

Varying from those norms in a classroom is sometimes possible—for example, a teacher might decide that eating in class is okay if students clean up afterward—but it's a good idea to know who might object and to work out the differences.

Follow up promptly and consistently on the agreed-upon expectations. Be honest and matter-of-fact when students break the rules, reminding them why they all agreed to them. If unacceptable behavior comes up that wasn't on the list, make clear why it detracts from the goals of the class. Warn offending students two or three times at most, then impose the appropriate consequence.

> Make sure that everything you do, you *can* do. If you're sending kids to the principal, make sure it really happens. If you're saying you're going to call the parents, do it, as long as there is a parent. MIKA

> She has this thing she says: If you're being an idiot, disrupting the class, you get a point taken off your final grade. But she doesn't do it anymore—she gave it up and she doesn't enforce it. Then it's unfair. BOSUNG

Practice the habits that create a good classroom tone. It's a teacher's responsibility as well as a student's to speak and act in ways that show mutual respect.

> Like when students are making trash in class, call students on it before the problem is really big. They may not notice they're doing the wrong thing. Don't make a big deal of it, do some of the work yourself. You would be part of helping keep it clean, and say something in a respectful but firm way. DIANA

> Don't say, "I already have a job, guys, you're the one that needs the education," or "I'm not getting paid to baby-sit you guys." I had one teacher who would just read the newspaper and wait until we got order ourselves. MIKA

If students are really learning, they will be asking questions all the time—in a manner that can sometimes annoy the teacher. Remember to treat questioning as a legitimate form of respectful speech, not a classroom misdemeanor.

Keep student learning as the top priority. Focus on teaching interesting and important material.

> Have something strong at the start [that] leads down the road to what you're teaching. We were prepared to get on my teacher [by giving him trouble], but he grabbed our attention from the start, and we were with him for the rest of the class. A kid can tell when a teacher knows what he's doing, and believes in what he's doing, then they don't have to get into some authority struggle. VANCE

> The worst thing you can do is start a class by saying everything that can't be done instead of saying everything that will try to be done throughout the year. DIANA

WHAT LIES BEHIND CLASSROOM DISRUPTIONS

Despite a teacher's best efforts, most will almost certainly face challenges from students who act in unacceptable ways. When that happens, remember that students are often trying to make a point when they disrupt a high school classroom.

> It's not that we're going to string teachers up, but most teenagers are insecure about something, and we'll take it out in different ways—we'll try to attack before they can attack us. VANCE

> Ask yourself what you're doing to make the problem worse, or even to cause it. That could stop the problem before it happens. MAHOGANY

The chart on page 42 illustrates how a teacher might "crack the code" of students' behavior to see its hidden message. Teachers can use it to address root causes, rather than simply imposing a punishment that could increase a student's alienation.

One behavior may carry a number of meanings. For example, students give a lot of reasons for putting their heads down on their desks: They may be physically ill, tired or sleepy, frustrated, angry or stressed, daydreaming, depressed, bored, or just confused.

> Sometimes students need to have their head down for a while. Sometimes I feel sick but I still go to school, because if I miss, it gets me stressed out for a week or two. MARIBEL

> If they don't know the answer, some students will crack jokes or disrupt to draw attention away from the fact. But I just put my head down and try to be quiet. VANCE

When we feel...	We act like this...	How a teacher could change that feeling
Unseen and unheard, resentful of the teacher-student power imbalance, disrespected or disliked by the teacher Anxious about not being able to do the work	Hostile or passive, refusing to participate or do work	Get to know us and our interests, hopes, and goals Create meaningful opportunities for us to express views and make decisions that affect us Arrange mediation for interpersonal conflicts between teacher and student
Bored	Inattentive, passing notes, playing cards, reading magazines, eating or drinking, talking to friends, giggling, pestering teacher with irrelevant questions	Use curriculum and activities that relate to our interests or call on our strengths
Physically restless Anxious about not being able to do the work	Physically disruptive, fighting, jittery, noisy, asking to go to the bathroom	Introduce more active, hands-on learning Call breaks to stretch or vocalize
Insecure about our status among peers	Smart-mouth attitude, swearing, challenging teacher's directions, making personal or cruel comments about teacher or peers	Remind students of agreed-upon ground rules Arrange mediation for interpersonal conflicts Give us leadership roles Ask us to help with others who are having problems
Upset or worried about personal or family troubles	Withdrawn, apathetic, inattentive, unfocused	Act and speak in a caring way Refer us for counseling

As a teenager I go through stuff that I don't think I should be going through—stuff I should be going through when I am an adult. Personal *and* school stuff. I don't work well under pressure. MONTOYA

My brother, he get bored by everything, he has a short attention span. I think a lot of boys have that. If it's a girl with her head down—most of the time they be like sick with girl stuff. They're more emotional. PORSCHE

Girls go through a lot of things in a month. They don't feel the same thing boys feel. Guys and girls think different—so teachers can act different in this situation. VERONICA

Many of these conditions are best addressed by a kind word or simple gesture:

The teacher should ask how is my day, am I okay, if he or she can help with the problem. Don't put the student on the spot and call their name out to say "Put your head up." If the teacher does that, I feel disrespected. MONTOYA

My teacher would touch me on the shoulder and ask, "Are you okay?" If I am, she would say, "I can't have you sleep in my class, so please step outside, rinse your face with cold water, then come back when you're okay." LAURALIZ

Usually the sleepiness goes around in the morning classes, when the heater's on, or when lights are off. My teacher always taps us on the shoulder when we fall asleep. ANDRES

But left unaddressed, the behavior takes its toll:

The class gets drained. You're taking attention from the teacher—you become more interesting than anything else. VANCE

> All I'm doing is taking a nap, and I'm getting lost even more. LAURALIZ

> I'm in a classroom and the teacher lets them put their heads down for a minute, pretty soon everyone will have their head down. TIFFANY

Take the trouble to figure out what's going on. When possible, doing something about it will make everyone feel better, not just the sleeper.

> If it looks like something is wrong, then one or two days with a couple of kids [with their heads down] is not too bad. At least they're in school. But if it's more than that, something's wrong with your class and you need to set it straight. BOSUNG

> Try to engage students if they're bored. MIKA

> [When I was confused] one teacher would kind of reassure me, look over my shoulder and lead me on the way: "Take it easy, you have it right there," or "You only have to do this." VANCE

Thinking this way about classroom disruptions can involve a shift in a teacher's whole approach toward students—away from thinking of them as problems to be controlled, and toward thinking of them as partners in achieving some common goals. For students to really believe this and respond with more positive behavior takes considerable trust, which is only built up over time, as teachers demonstrate their own commitment to fairness and respect.

WHAT'S FAIR AND WHAT'S NOT

Of course, setting a good classroom tone also involves stopping disruptions when they happen. But students need to know that teachers are acting fairly when they call students on unacceptable behavior. They watch for these things:

Listen to both sides and establish the facts.

Punishment for something you're not responsible for will ruin the student-teacher relationship, easy as that. Make sure you have the facts, all of them. Say what you know and no more. Don't stretch the truth. I think the principal automatically assumes that the teacher is right.
ANDRES

If you aren't sure of something, you can't blame just anybody. You really have to look carefully into the problem. I have gotten in trouble a few times for supposedly talking in class, but the teacher got me confused with somebody else who was talking. I almost got a referral for arguing with the teacher because he said I would have to stay after class. DIANA

Don't make assumptions. When I was in eighth grade I had a history teacher who I did not like and she apparently did not like me either. When she turned her back, this girl sitting next to me called her a jerk. She turned around and threw me out of my class for saying it, and she gave me detention and said she would check if I was there, and she would give me detention for the whole week. The girl never admitted it.
TIFFANY

IDENTIFYING THE ASSETS OF YOUR WORST-BEHAVING STUDENTS

Looking carefully at other sides of a student's life can often give a teacher insight into disruptive behavior in the classroom and how to prevent or stop it. Try answering these questions for any student whose behavior causes a problem. (If you don't know the answers, talk to other teachers to find out.) **Important note:** Keep these notes in a secure place to ensure students' privacy!

Name of the troublemaker: _____

What do you know about this student's school experiences outside your class?

*Interest or performance in other courses?*_____

_____

*Aspirations or information about further schooling?*_____

_____

What do you know about this student's life or special challenges outside school?

*Jobs?*_____

_____

Family responsibilities? _____

_____

*Social connections (church, gang, neighborhood)?*_____

_____

Commute to school (distance and time, walks, takes bus from another neighborhood)?

_____

What strengths or skills must this student have in order to function in that life outside school? Mark all that apply, adding your notes or thoughts:

Organization and planning experience _____

Ability to collaborate in a group effort _____

Leadership ability _____

Persistence _____

Other (describe) _____

In what ways does your classroom already recognize or call on this student's existing skills?

_____

_____

In what ways might you connect those skills to the work and purposes of your class?

_____

_____

What more could you do to build a positive connection with this student?

_____

_____

Treat students consistently, but also as individuals. Don't play favorites, alienating some kids to be friendly with others.

> My friend and I had got through with our work and we were bored, so we started talking, and our teacher kicked my friend out. After she left, there were students still talking, and he didn't say anything to them. That was unfair. MAHOGANY

> Teachers think blacks are the loud ones and so they always pick on them—say some Hispanics and some black girls are talking, they tell only the black girls to be quiet. It just makes them mad. Black girls get buck wild, but in the classroom they know when to act right. Some people just naturally talk loud. PORSCHE

> One group of kids gets into trouble and the school doesn't bother to distinguish between them when punishing them—they all just get lumped together as one entity. HILARY

Don't overreact. The behavior may not arise from defiance but from some less disrespectful cause, like trying to fit in with peers. Don't take it to higher-ups or parents before speaking with the student.

> Teachers need to realize that referrals are for really disruptive students they can't handle, not for silly stuff. Referrals go on your record; they make copies and send them home. And sometimes teachers misuse the referrals; they don't realize how much they affect us. MAHOGANY

Recognize that there's a time for quiet and other times when students need to talk together. The pace and rhythm of a class can respond to both needs without a teacher's "losing control."

> Some teachers try to keep the class quiet, but it has to be everybody quiet—and that's just a waste of time. If they would just teach, people would be quiet enough. It's only important to a certain extent. DIANA

Make time to listen to students. If a student continues to act in troubling ways, ask in private what's behind the behavior. Be aware that other students may also be exerting pressure on the student. Try to find common ground or a way out of a bad cycle. Be willing to revisit previous actions in light of what is revealed.

> Sometimes the teachers have also used bad language to the students, or done something disrespectful that provokes a student to swear or act bad. LAURALIZ

> One student says nasty things to me and I start crying at home. My teachers should intervene, even if I say I don't want them to. LAURALIZ

> One teacher I had last year had a lot of conferences with me. I'm never going to like her, but at least we could agree to respect each other—she would treat me like everyone else. DIANA

DECIDING ON CONSEQUENCES

What is the right consequence for inappropriate behavior? Students agree that teachers should use their judgment to find something that fits the person and the situation. Remember to keep student *learning* as the ultimate goal of every consequence.

> You want to give them something they don't want to do, but also you want them to learn from it. They should have a place with something to do, like write an essay and present it to the school, or do community service to help people. LUIS

Or write an apology letter, or clean the streets. Even if you don't give the same punishment to everyone, it's okay as long as you explain it. VERONICA

But you don't want to make it so they lose all their interest and motivation to work hard, get better, and do well. ANDRES

Some things don't warrant going to the principal's office, so teachers can be inventive about the consequences.

If they like to write notes in class, they can stand at the board and take notes for the class. PORSCHE

Shame them, but only to a limit. Our egos are fragile, we're insecure, but we can take things like making us a little butt of a joke. Whatever they did, make them do something contrary or ironic to that—make them overdo it. MIKA

Don't cross that line into insulting a student by the way you talk to them—the line can be fuzzy. ALEXIS

Handle everyday offenses (talking, note-passing, horseplay, rowdiness) within the classroom with a stern voice or a powerful glare.

Move the kids to separate sides of the room, or have them sit in front or back of the class and look stupid. MIKA

Don't read notes out loud—it might be about you. Or it might be harmful to students to have them shared. MARIBEL

Directly address and condemn the behavior itself, not the person doing it, treating kids like they have a sense of responsibility.

> Point out exactly what they are doing—you can't argue with that. Use common sense: "Come on, we have to be here together for another hour. How are you helping yourself by acting that way?" LATIA

Occasionally a surprise move makes the point best, but physical force is never an option.

> Catch our attention with a quick flashy action—drop your book and sit there in silence looking at us like: Are you ready to learn? VANCE

As a last resort, ask students to leave the class for a period of time, as long as school policy permits this. Emphasize that both teacher and student have a responsibility to support the learning of the entire class.

> Say: "If you want to be a joker, don't do it here. Don't come back if you want to disrupt the class. I'm not going to have it in my area." ALEXIS

> There's no way you can make a kid to do something, but make clear that you can get them in trouble. LAURALIZ

Don't leave the class yourself to show your disapproval of student behavior. They need your consistent message that you will work through such problems as a group.

Some behavior, such as touching or physically threatening a teacher or other students, is so offensive or dangerous that the first offense warrants immediate removal of the student from the class.

Conflicts between students can also be serious. Deal with mean or disrespectful comments in the classroom as they occur, and refer students for mediation right away. If fighting breaks out, school and district policy usually takes the consequence—probably suspension—out of a teacher's hands.

Teachers need to be aware that certain students irk each other. ALEXIS

Teenagers might not want the teacher to protect them. I feel worse if I can't protect myself. LUIS

That's why it's better to [talk about disrespect] in the classroom. But outside the class, you have to somehow help the victim get some skills in protecting themselves. HILARY

Student co-authors from Oakland analyzed the pros and cons of different kinds of sanctions in the chart on page 53.

WHAT'S AN EFFECTIVE CONSEQUENCE?

Sanction	What's good about it	What's bad about it
Community service; helping people	They get a chance to help people instead of hurting people	Might not relate to the offense; removes them from school environment
Cleaning the streets and highways; planting trees	They work together in teams; benefit to the community	Might not relate to the offense; removes them from school environment
Taking away privileges like field trips or senior perks	They get their grades up and learn their lesson	If they can't go on a field trip, they lose their motivation and interest in learning
Writing an essay about the offense	Makes the student think about the issue; uses writing to express ideas	Students don't take it seriously
Calling parents	Shows that you take it seriously; involves family in the solution	Too extreme for many situations; you alienate the student
Peer mediation	Brings students into the solution; creates pressure from peers	Some situations too serious for peers to handle; confidentality issues
Detention or enforced study hall	At least they are working on schoolwork	They get the message that schoolwork is punishment
Suspension (not the teacher's decision to impose)	You remove them from the situation where they're making trouble	You lose the chance to supervise them and help them learn

COMMON MISTAKES AND HELPFUL TIPS

Don't joke with students until you know them very well. MARIBEL

Don't act scared.
Teachers don't need to be scared of children. Don't let us intimidate you.
When you let your student walk all over you, they're not learning the essentials
of respect, of how to interact properly. ALEXIS

**Don't ignore disrespectful or disruptive behavior. Respond matter-of-factly
but firmly the first time someone acts in an unacceptable way.**
Say: "If you want to be a joker, don't do it here. Don't come back if you want
to disrupt the class. I'm not going to have it in my area." ALEXIS

Don't confuse overly personal comments by students with their liking you.
Some kids try to get a young teacher to talk about her boyfriend, just to
embarrass her. TIFFANY

**Don't put on an artificial mask of either meanness to win respect or smiles
to win approval; just be yourself.**
One teacher puts a big smile on her face for everything, even taking the trash
out. LAURALIZ

Don't let it go if a student doesn't do the homework.
If you know the kid and he suddenly stops, pay attention, because there's
something wrong. DIANA

Do something fun and active with students in the first few days of school.
Our math teacher gave us puzzles. LAURALIZ

Don't overuse "please."
If you say "please" too much, they think it's an option. DARYL

Remember to give students physical breaks from sitting and working.
I had this teacher who made us get up and scream this funny word two or three times to get us going. MARIBEL

I hate that! There's a class that does that next door and I'm sitting right next to it and it's awful. What are you doing! We're trying to learn! It's definitely not helping my learning. BOSUNG

Keep an eye out for all students, not just the rowdy ones.
Teachers pay attention to the loud kids, but often it's the quiet kids that they should watch out for. DIANA

Don't let kids pick on and laugh at another kid.
You can tell when it's okay, when they're friends with each other, but a teacher should know when it's inappropriate. MAHOGANY

But remember, the kid may not understand how mean it is. Make a place where he can learn to understand it. DARYL

Don't call on people just to make them pay attention.
It makes them feel bad, and then they stop paying attention even more. If they're not paying attention or if they're talking with each other too much, sit them in front or split them up somehow. PORSCHE

Don't let them work with their friends all the time.
If they're gonna sit me with my friends, I'm gonna start talking: What you gonna do for lunch? VERONICA

Sometimes they should get to [work with friends]. If they know each other well, they could start a good argument about a subject. LUIS

Sometimes it's good to work with friends, especially with work outside of school, like going to the library or projects. Because you can call your friends and have them over to your house and get it done. You're not gonna do that if you don't know the person. PORSCHE

WHAT ABOUT CALLING PARENTS?

Keeping up good communication with families definitely boosts student learning, but most teenagers have mixed responses to their teachers' calling their parents when they cause trouble in class. They consider it more respectful to work out most behavior issues directly with them.

> When you're older, there's a lot of reasons a teacher shouldn't call home for anything under a suspension-level thing. It's a trust issue—it's like betrayal. ANDRES

> Whether or not we choose to utilize what school has to offer is something that should be discussed between student and teacher—not parents, students, and teachers. MIKA

They may already have conflicts at home that could be made worse by a call from a teacher.

> If you get suspended, aren't your parents just gon' hit you more? PORSCHE

> Jamaican values are so different and if you don't understand them, it's hard to explain. For a kid to say, "I can't bring home this 80 to my parents," most people are like, "What are you talking about! Take it and go home." MIKA

> If they don't have a good relationship with the parent, call the guardian or someone the student trusts—maybe a grandparent. LUIS

Yet students do recognize that a strong relationship between school and family, even in the teenage years, supports success in school. To forge that relationship successfully, a high school teacher must first clearly understand the student's home situation so as to know whether, how, and when to include the family in the dialogue about a student's development. Chapter 1 of this book offers some basic techniques for getting to that understanding. Make clear from the beginning which circumstances will require you to contact the parent or guardian. And don't hesitate to ask a student directly what would be the best route to involving a caring family member.

THE SPECIAL PROBLEM OF SUBSTITUTES

Almost all high school students try to get away with murder when a substitute teacher takes their class. Partly this reflects resentment at having what often amounts to a baby-sitter who knows neither the subject nor the students.

> They should be trained! My teacher had surgery and we had substitutes for two months. They were just, like, reading a newspaper. I stopped going to that class—we weren't doing anything anyway, so we're just, like, throwing things in the hall. LUIS

> A substitute should only be teaching something they know—they shouldn't just put them anywhere. That's just wasting our day! You'd learn more at home. MONTOYA

> In math class last year we had like eighteen substitutes. One teacher would try telling us one thing and the next would tell you another thing. I stopped going to that class because I wasn't learning anything. VERONICA

Students suggest various alternatives:

> Get feedback on the substitute, and get the ones that work well to come back. VERONICA

> Our school has a substitute who knows us—she's like the school's substitute. She knows all kinds of subjects. LUIS

A teacher should always prepare a detailed lesson plan for a substitute teacher, including as much detail as possible about the class. Give copies to the students, too, so everyone agrees.

> If kids are going to be working in groups at tables, name who's in the groups and who the table leaders are. MONTOYA

CLOTHING AS A BEHAVIOR ISSUE

Teenagers care a lot about what they wear, and they don't like it when that choice is subject to school rules and disciplinary action.

> Don't be obsessed with what kids are wearing. It's so far from what you need to worry about, it's just not the issue. When I was in eighth grade our principal thought that all the school's problems were because the girls were wearing revealing clothes. They wouldn't let us wear tank tops. You shouldn't assume things based on people's clothing. It's inappropriate and offensive; they weren't treating us like humans. HILARY

> If you are going to worry about the clothes, worry about the things that are important, not the do-rags boys tie on their heads. I don't think there are so many things that a teacher should pay attention to. DIANA

At the same time, kids realize that individual teachers don't make school rules on clothes and must enforce them whether they want to or not.

> It's not whether you enforce the rules, it's how you talk to students. A teacher could say: "It's not my rule, and I don't necessarily agree with it, but you know that it is against the rule." If a teacher comes at you that way, you don't lose respect for the rule, but if they come at you yelling, it makes you not care, not have respect. MAHOGANY

When clothing rules relate to gang colors or symbols, as they often do, the situation gets more complicated still.

> When students come in with a lot of red on [an indicator of gang alle-giance], teachers have to get on their case because it makes the teachers not look good if the students are not following the rules in their class-rooms. They refer them to the office and then they have to call home.
> ANDRES

Students often have a sure sense of what signifies and what doesn't in clothing:

> There's people who wear blue every day, but I know for a fact that they're not in a gang. Usually you can kind of tell—especially if they're hanging out with a lot of people who are wearing the same color. But it's not a for-sure thing. It might be a coincidence. ANDRES

They also spot gang signals that go right over the heads of teachers.

> It's always smaller things. Last week we had a big problem with [the gangs] *norteños* and *sureños*, and it was because of their belts. The teach-ers didn't even notice the belts. DIANA

> The longer the belt is, and its color, signal a lot about their gang status, so teachers need to pay attention to it. We have this mural, and it has a gang hand signal up there. I don't know why they don't notice it! But I do.
> ANDRES

Talking to students is the best way for teachers to educate themselves about the gang presence in their school, students agree.

That's how they stay up on a lot of stuff. Unless you know kids, you won't know what their gang allegiance is, if they have one. Most students at least know somebody that's in some gang, but the majority is not in one. DIANA

Teachers should pay attention to what they hear and see, but not rush to conclusions or exaggerate the danger that may exist at school.

I know a lot of people who belong to different sets, but they come to school as a way of leaving that all behind. If they were out with their friends on the weekends they might not get along, but at school it's neutral. MAHOGANY

It's more about claiming their streets and their blocks than claiming their color at school. DIANA

Though students regard fights as unacceptable, they also don't like to see armed police officers at school, which sends the message that students are dangerous people.

They overdo it. Two or three girls were fighting, and they brought a paddy wagon and weapons. Kids were all looking out of the window. The whole school was distracted. MAHOGANY

THE COMMON SENSE OF CLASSROOM MANAGEMENT

All the stern discipline in the world can't keep teenagers from sabotaging a classroom where they don't feel any personal involvement. Common sense suggests that a teacher spend energy on generating class work and approaches that interest and engage students, rather than trying to act as a baby-sitter or guard.

Though a certain amount of push-and-pull behavior inevitably shows up in groups of adolescents and adults, the payoff for high engagement always includes a positive classroom culture. In the next several chapters, we explore the ways in which teachers can draw students into a genuine partnership in their learning.

Summary
FOSTERING POSITIVE CLASSROOM BEHAVIOR

- Let us know your plan for the class.

- Work with us on expectations for classroom behavior.

- Follow up promptly and consistently on the agreed-upon expectations.

- Keep student learning as the top priority.

- When trouble occurs, keep an open mind and establish the facts.

- Treat us consistently, but also as individuals.

- Recognize that there's a time for quiet and other times when we need to talk.

- Make time to listen to us.

CHAPTER 4

Creating a Culture of Success

"HE JUST PUSHED ME TO KEEP MY HEAD OUTA THEM BOYS AND INTO THE BOOKS."

Teachers show that they value and respect students partly by letting them know that they hold high expectations for them, as students observed in Chapter 2. And just as with respect, those expectations apply to both teacher and student. Teachers can make the bargain perfectly clear: They will provide schoolwork that really matters, along with the support students need to succeed at it. In return, students will give their best effort to master important knowledge and skills.

This bargain requires considerable trust on both sides. Students will sometimes have to take on faith that difficult or seemingly irrelevant academic material "really matters." And teachers will have to believe in what their students can do, even when real-life stresses make their "best efforts" fall short. But if trust has built up between them in the ways described in our first three chapters, the high expectations can pay off on both sides. Adolescent students do not always make school a top priority. They may be spending most of their time figuring out their own identities as young adults. They may be using their energy to cross daily barriers of language and culture. Negative experiences in the classroom may have convinced them that school offers nothing worthwhile, or that they won't ever fit into its neat categories.

> They shouldn't expect me always to do good. Sometimes you go through lots of stuff—if something happens in your family you might not be going to school—and you don't know when that is going to be. It's important

for a teacher to let you know that even if you don't do the very best this time, they still expect that you'll be able to in the future. VERONICA

If you don't do the work, she won't give you the makeup work. She doesn't realize she's being unfair to us. She's sending us the signal that it's okay with her if we don't learn. She'll be like, "It's going to be late anyway, so don't turn it in." Then when she does the grade, she takes off for it anyway. She don't want you there, or something. PORSCHE

But if a teacher keeps believing in their value and their ability, kids are willing to try, and try again.

My tenth-grade bio-science teacher had faith in me when all my other teachers thought I was a lost cause. He told me, "I know you're smart when you want to be. You just have to want to do it." He prepared me for what it's going to be like in college and in the eleventh grade. PORSCHE

When my adviser called me and said I should come back to the school [after not doing well the first year], he gave me the signal that he expected me to try hard and do well. My school is about giving second chances— they thought I could do better and they invited me to go back. ANDRES

When teachers consistently give this message, a culture of success begins to develop in the class and the school.

In my school there's no one that's better [than anyone else]—we're all trying to graduate. You can stop a teacher and ask a question any time. MIKA

SHOWING BELIEF IN STUDENTS

What specific signals can teachers send to show students they expect them to try hard and do well? Student co-authors have these suggestions:

Remind us often that you expect our best. Be friendly and understanding, but keep pushing us. Show that you value our participation by asking us questions in class.

> My English and history teacher is very understanding and nice. He always pushes me farther. I wouldn't even think I could do something, and he would push me, and I would succeed, and do really well. MONTOYA

> If a teacher doesn't think you're smart, they won't call on you. They'll pay you very little attention. MAHOGANY

> It's okay for your teachers to push you—it just shows they care and they want to see you succeed in life. PORSCHE

Encourage our efforts even if we are having trouble. Don't disparage or shame us when we don't get things right away.

> My teacher pushes me to work hard instead of giving up. She doesn't tell you it's old work and you should know the answer. MAHOGANY

> We had to do math problems in groups, and each day some students had to go up and present them. If you weren't 100 percent sure, you wouldn't want to. I thought I knew it and I presented it and I was wrong. It was a terrible feeling, but the teacher did a good job of helping me get the right answer while I was up there, so I didn't have to go sit down and let someone else explain it. He asked a couple of questions that helped me understand why what I did was wrong. HILARY

Teenagers care about what other people think of them, and so they feel intimidated. ALEXIS

Give helpful feedback and expect us to revise.

> If they don't expect you to do well, they'll give you a check minus but they won't tell you what you did wrong—so you keep on doing it and getting bad grades. Some teachers take the time to tell you—say I write an essay and I misplace a paragraph—so next time you won't make the same mistake. It's less like a grade and more like advice for next time. It makes you feel like she expects you to do well. VERONICA

> You know they expect you to do well when you write something and they write comments on it—even if they talk smart and it's upsetting. MONTOYA

> Like when they use red and write in big letters—I don't want no one hollering at me on paper! Still, it shows they care. PORSCHE

> My English teacher takes his time and gives clear advice on what you did right. He'll say, "I know you know how to do this, but you must have forgotten it that time." LUIS

Give us plenty of support along the way. Don't leave it to the final presentation to tell us how to improve. Make yourself available for help, and set up tutoring sessions if we need them.

> My algebra teacher, when I got a C in his class, he was upset. He just pushed me to keep my head outa them boys and into the books. He made me go to tutoring after school to keep my grades up. PORSCHE

If they expect you to do well, they give you their email addresses in case you need them. They tell you to come in for tutoring. MAHOGANY

Help us set priorities among the different things we do. Remember, your class is just one of the many obligations we have.

This kid had a lot of teachers who liked him; he was a good basketball player and they were pulling him in different directions. It can be bad. VANCE

Don't favor the students you think will do the best. Call on students equally in class. Push everybody to improve, and acknowledge signs of improvement right away.

I have a teacher who pushes the "good" students a lot more than the not-so-good students. Like when a straight-A student doesn't do the work he'll give that person lectures and whatnot, but when a lower-grade student doesn't do the work he'll just give up, like he didn't expect it anyway. DIANA

If a teacher doesn't respond, or dismisses it when you raise your hand to make a comment, that's a signal that she expects you to fail. It's a self-fulfilling prophecy. My little sister had one English teacher where she's always gotten Cs and Ds and even though she's trying hard now, she's getting the same grades. HILARY

When my teacher doesn't expect you to try hard or do anything, they won't say anything to you or call on you. One teacher, if he doesn't think you are smart, he won't call on you. LAURALIZ

Don't compare us to other students.

> The worst thing a teacher can do is to compare a class to another class, and put them down. My third-period chemistry teacher said things like, "My first-period class got that, I don't see why you don't get it."
> MAHOGANY

> Most students do not want to be singled out—praise and criticism feel almost the same. BOSUNG

Stick with us. It's hard for kids to believe we'll succeed if our teachers give up on us. When teachers quit, it sends a message that we aren't worth the trouble, and if a teacher doesn't care enough to stick with it, why should we?

TEACHING STUDENTS TO TAKE RISKS

Taking a risk in class—by offering an opinion, venturing an answer without being sure, or showing what they know or can do—is especially hard for teenagers, who care so much what their peers think of them.

> Intimidation is invisible to a teacher in a classroom. They can't necessarily see that for whatever subject it is, every student often adds extra pressure to ourselves in our minds—not wanting to be picked on, people will make fun of you, you don't have the right answer. These are all the things that run through your mind, and your teacher doesn't know that that's the way you feel. ALEXIS

> Sometimes a student feels like they have to know everything about a question to ask a question about it. You only feel comfortable if you know enough about the question to ask the question. VANCE

REVISING AND REFLECTION: Basic Work Tools of a Culture of Success

Teaching students the habit of revising their work goes further than any other single strategy for success. Even if a student does good work the first time, it can always get better in revision. And if the work falls short the first time, we feel better about trying again when the teacher expects everyone to do serious revision, not just those who didn't do well.

When students reflect on their work process after finishing a paper or project, they also get in the habit of believing in their own ability to succeed. Spelling out what they did well, and how to improve, reminds them that learning is a continuous process, not a win-or-lose deal.

Make revision and reflection a normal part of every major paper or project you assign. Here are two worksheets you can give students at the appropriate times.

For Revision: A Worksheet to Give to Students

What do I still need to find out in order to improve this work?

_____

How can I get the information and help I need?

_____

What steps do I need to take to revise?

_____

On_____ [this day], gather information on this:

_____

On_____ [this day], get help from these people:

_____

By_____ [this day], work again on this part:

_____

By_____ [this day], work again on this part:

_____

For Reflection: A Worksheet to Give Students

In terms of...	Worked well because...	Could improve by...
How I used my time on this assignment		
How I worked with others on this assignment		
Asking for help when needed		
How I presented what I learned		

Teachers can help by encouraging students' contributions to build on each other, so that learning becomes the whole group's task. By concentrating on open-ended questions that require real thinking, teachers can avoid the impression that the "right" answers matter more than others.

> Maybe in the beginning of the year or when you start class, say to students in a reassuring way: If you don't know the answer, it's okay; if you do, it's okay. ALEXIS

> It's good when a teacher allows you to fail, and accepts something even though it's not right but you're on the road to something right. There's a lot of pressure on high schoolers to get it right or not hand it in, because you think it's stupid. VANCE

> In our math class the teacher expected us to present our answers on the board. One time I wrote the wrong answer up, but I still felt safe to participate because he found a way to turn it into a correct answer. HILARY

All students, however, do not come to a class discussion with the same background information. Students with different upbringings probably will not share the same reference points of history, literature, film, or other cultural narratives. Be alert for silence, distraction, or little signs of confusion that might indicate this unfamiliarity. And without drawing attention to any particular student, provide a brief explanation to prevent a conversation from excluding them. Teachers can also invite the class to enrich the conversation with references that are more familiar to them.

> Teachers assume you know what they're talking about; they assume that you'll ask if you have a problem. I don't know what *Schindler's List* is. ALEXIS

He's talking about a movie and they're laughing, and you're like shaking your head and saying *mmm*. But you don't know about it. LAURALIZ

Even when a teacher expects you to ask questions, they don't really back it up with actions. When you're talking about history and everyone is having a good time and you don't get a certain thing, you don't want to be the one who's asking the question. VANCE

Whether or not they know the material, many students feel painfully reluctant to draw attention to themselves. Stay alert to possible openings.

Every student wants to feel special and smart and talented, but at the same time we want to blend in. So when we make that little effort to raise our hand—and it takes a lot of effort to, like, stand out—we need you to see it, and more than seeing it, to seek it. And if we stutter a little bit, and have trouble getting it out, don't be quick with us, but support us. VANCE

Teachers can speak privately to students having trouble, and without humiliating them explain their expectations and help them find ways to meet them.

I don't like when people stare in my grill. My teacher came to me and said: "I understand your frustration, but I'm not going to leave you alone. You have to write down what you have to say, so that by the time we get to you, you have something to say and you won't have to make anyone wait and look at you." So now that's what I do, and it was one of the most important things I ever learned in my high school career. MIKA

Like if I couldn't get what I wanted out, I would just say "Forget it"—but [that teacher] was like, "You know what you want to say, take your time." It would be silence, and I could feel everyone looking at me, so I would

say, "Forget it, forget it." After class he would take me aside and say, "You're really smart, you have a lot to say, so take your time and say it."
ALEXIS

When certain students get labeled as the ones who participate, nobody benefits.

I'm working extra hard to know all the answers, and I'm then having to work extra hard so the other kids don't punish me for knowing all the answers. For the sake of the class running smoothly, you have to have someone to answer the question, but why every day! I think I've been a crutch for the teacher in at least 85 percent of my classes. I like knowing things, but whether or not I know it shouldn't make or break your class.
LATIA

Finally, keep a close eye on whether students are turning in their homework.

Don't let it go if a student doesn't do the homework. If you know the kid and he suddenly stops, pay attention. DIANA

I give up on my test or homework because I don't understand it, and when the teacher comes around to collect it, I put it in my book bag and they don't notice. LAURALIZ

OTHER PRESSURES STUDENTS FEEL

A teacher's expectations are not the only pressure students feel when it comes to doing well in school. In deciding how hard to work, teenagers may also be responding to the values and priorities of friends, family, the culture that surrounds them outside of school, and their own internal feelings of pride in a job well done. Don't oversimplify this complex and shifting mix.

Compliments don't make me want to achieve. The feeling of accomplishment pressures me to do well. My own motivation is enough—I see the results of not doing so good. ANDRES

You could be a good student and not be popular. But I don't think you're cool for getting bad grades. It's the things you do that make your grades fall that are cool. MAHOGANY

So what if you want to do your homework! Have confidence, *be* dorky with your big salary and your Lexus cars. If I knew in eighth or ninth grade what I know now, I would have been busting those grades down without a fail, doing all my work, and certain things would have turned out differently. You don't have to be an overachiever—just get it done. ALEXIS

For a teenager it's not always about doing what everybody else does. Sometimes kids find their identity by standing out from the crowd.

At my other school a lot of people didn't achieve, and if you slack off you become a common person, blurred in the teacher's eyes. But if you go to a school where the class GPA is over 3.0, if you slack off you would be more popular—because you're doing the opposite. ANDRES

Sometimes students avoid doing well to gain the acceptance of peers. But just as often, acceptance relates more to other factors than school performance.

How people see you—it shouldn't be a reason but it is. I know a person that missed the last five questions on the SAT just so she wouldn't get a perfect score. ANDRES

I sometimes put pressure on my friend not to do well. I called her a square girl because she gets better grades. At that moment I had anger inside of me. I didn't think. VERONICA

"I DON'T GET IT": An Exercise for Teachers

Almost all of us have moments when we just don't understand something. It's not always in school; sometimes it's a joke we don't get, a place we can't find even with directions, or a confusing new electronic device. Thinking back through your own experience can help you identify with what your students may be going through. (You might also do and discuss this exercise with students, but leave out the last two questions.)

Describe one time you just didn't understand something:

_____

_____

Who else was there?

_____

_____

Did anyone react in a way that made it worse? If so, describe it here:

_____

_____

How did you feel when that happened?

_____

_____

Did anyone react in a way that helped you out? If so, describe it here:

_____

_____

How did you feel when that happened?

_____

_____

What did you wish someone would do to help?

_____

_____

Does the situation you experienced remind you of any student's situation in your class? If so, describe it:

_____

_____

What might you do to help?

_____

_____

I used to cut school a lot and get bad grades, and hang around with different people, who were like "come with us, do this, do that." Now, since I don't cut as much, they've accepted me as a better student, and so the same people who were giving me pressure before not to do well are now almost like pressure to do well. DIANA

Pressures from family can take various forms. Many students get more pressure to help out with child care, housework, or earnings than they do to excel at school. Others feel that their family's pressure has more to do with a parent's agenda than with the student's best interests.

All of my cousins went to good colleges, and because my other two sisters didn't go to college, that's pressure, too. Especially because my mom and dad are divorced. On my dad's side they're successful in business, in sports—and my mom wants me to show my father I can be successful. It's a big battle between them, but it's affecting me. MAHOGANY

Having a straight-A older sister puts a lot of pressure on me to do better than what I do. DIANA

My mother always expected me to study hard and one day work in a job that pays a lot of money. I grew up thinking I wanted to be a doctor. One day my mom found me drawing instead of studying. She got mad at me, thinking I was slacking off and being lazy not doing my homework. Her expectation of me changed when she realized I didn't want to be a wealthy person. She then expected me to study hard but to do it because I wanted to and not because I wanted to someday be rich. I was allowed to draw after I finished my homework. After the discussion, my mom changed her expectation and made it to being me getting high grades so that in the future I could get into any college and study anything I wanted to study. MARIBEL

My parents have always had expectations of me to try my best in school. I had to get decent grades in order to please them, or so I thought. I was very pressured and it is, in fact, a very difficult thing to do one's best. Of course, it is close to impossible to come home every day with an A or A+ on a paper or test, so I have not "met" their expectations, but I found later that my parents weren't expecting perfect scores but just that I try hard. BOSUNG

Even when teenagers are excruciatingly aware that they are the first in their families to graduate, they may feel conflicting pressures from parents and siblings.

My brother who didn't graduate makes me feel like I'm dumb—he puts pressure on me to not do well because he didn't. He's like: "How you gonna graduate? I told you if I didn't graduate they not going to graduate you either." VERONICA

My older brother didn't graduate from high school. If you're going to be the first one to graduate and go to college, your parents are wanting you to get good grades. I have a brother right behind me and he's looking up to me, so that's a lot of pressure. MONTOYA

My brothers and sisters are like, "She got bad grades, so why don't I?" PORSCHE

GRADES, PRAISE, AND OTHER INCENTIVES

By high school, teenagers see grades as a powerful and personal judgment on who they are and what the future will hold. For most, grades play a large part in forming their self-image. A bad grade can feel like a blow from which they can't recover; a good grade can boost their energy and motivation.

> I hurt when I get a bad grade! You feel like you're doing all that hard work for nothing. Then you don't want to work more, if you're just going to get bad grades. Whenever my grades get low I feel like dropping out of school. PORSCHE

> I hated school all this year because my grades are pretty low. No matter how much I try, they are still the same. The one time I loved school was in the fifth grade when I got straight As on my report card. That was the most wonderful day. VERONICA

> I have loved school very few times, but it would be either because our team won a game or my grades were up. DIANA

Adolescents have a passion for justice, and it matters a lot to them that their grades are fair, whether they turn out high or low.

> In middle school I would make people show me their homework so I could copy it. When the teachers started to notice my answers were the same, I started to realize that I wouldn't get anywhere unless I did my own work. My grades would come after the test and I would get an F. And I started to change. That happened because the teacher noticed and kept a close eye. VERONICA

> I had a teacher that taught math and chemistry and didn't know either

HOW DO I GRADE?

How you go about grading can contribute substantially to creating a classroom culture of success. Before you assess any piece of student work, and also before you decide on the final grade for the course, ask yourself the following questions:

Have I clearly stated (preferably using assessment rubrics) what criteria the student's work must meet to qualify for a particular grade:

☐ In terms of work completed?

☐ In terms of work habits (participation, collaboration, drafts, revisions)?

☐ In terms of content mastery?

Notes:

_____

_____

Have I given students the support they need to meet each of those criteria:

☐ In terms of work completed?

☐ In terms of work habits?

☐ In terms of content mastery?

Notes:

_____

_____

What more could I do in the future to make this student's success more likely?

_____

_____

What other feedback can I give to this student besides a letter grade?

_____

_____

one. If you were quiet you got an A, and if you were talking you wouldn't do well. It was good getting an A in that class, but when I go to college it will be a punishment for me. I'll be stuck. MAHOGANY

Even if they don't meet the standard, they want to be acknowledged or even rewarded if they have tried hard at something.

Some teachers don't give you good grades for work that you try hard for, because they say you could have done better. DIANA

You want to know that when you work hard it will be rewarded or acknowledged. If teachers don't pay enough attention to know when a student has really put in some extra effort, then I don't think that students will try hard—because what difference does it make? HILARY

Direct and specific feedback from the teacher helps kids much more than grades.

If instead of grades we just had a paper from the teacher telling us how we are doing, we would want more to go back and do it better. PORSCHE

You don't need to have grades to want to work harder. If my teachers told me how I was doing without grades, I would pay attention to it. You want to know how you're doing, but you don't want to feel bad about yourself. Just say: I want you to do this, this, this, and this. They would be treating us more with respect. VERONICA

But that feedback should remain a private thing. You can find positive ways (like peer editing of written pieces) for having students share and critique each other's work. Making students' grades public, however, creates especially bad feelings.

WHAT DO I EXPECT OF STUDENTS, AND HOW DO I SHOW IT?

Sometimes teachers don't realize the ways in which they are sending messages to students about how well they expect them to perform. Use this exercise to analyze a sample of your own students (including two who usually receive Bs), noting their strengths and limitations:

Student's name	Usual Grade	Strengths	Limitations
	A		
	B		
	B		
	C		
	D		

Now think about the A student you listed above. Can you imagine yourself ever giving this student a D? If that feels unlikely, explain why.

What might you do if this student suddenly began to perform badly?

_____

_____

Now think about the D student you listed above. Can you imagine yourself ever giving this student an A? If that feels unlikely, explain why.

_____

_____

How might you react if this student suddenly began to turn in A-level work?

_____

_____

Now look over the strengths and limitations of all the students you listed. How do you reinforce their strengths and help them overcome their limitations?

_____

_____

Some techniques you can use with all *your students:*

- Ask them what question they can be prepared to answer in class the next day.
- Listen in a way that respects and acknowledges their response.
- Encourage them to ask questions and treat their questions as important.
- Encourage and model follow-up questions. ("How might that change if . . . ?")
- Set up a meeting with the student to find out background issues or give support.
- Ask their thoughts on an open-ended question that matters to them. ("What do you think about what happened yesterday?")
- Acknowledge their good work or helpful contribution.
- Respond to something in the student's writing.

Trading tests to correct them is embarrassing sometimes. We have a lot of students who can barely speak English, and [the teacher] would call out, "Who got them all right? Who got less than 10?" And everyone knew what you got. It's okay to correct it like that, but you shouldn't say it out loud. DIANA

When other people graded our paper and passed it back to us, he looked at it privately and didn't call out the grades. Except he did tell one student: "You were the only person in both classes who got a perfect all week." If you get a 49 out of 50 he won't say anything, so it makes you feel stupid. ANDRES

Teenagers are also often sensitive to being embarrassed in front of others by public praise or criticism.

I know the other person's gonna hate me when I get praise and someone else doesn't. VERONICA

When the teacher tells me what I did wrong in front of the class, I feel very bad and like I am not capable. But I don't mind being singled out for praise. MONTOYA

It feels nice when a teacher singles me out for praise because it lets everyone know I am smart. When a teacher singles me out for criticism, it feels really bad because people think you're dumb and can't do anything. PORSCHE

Grades and praise are not the only incentives that matter. Kids realize that learning has its own rewards—intellectual, pragmatic, and psychological.

If you can read, you can do anything. I didn't learn that because I was supposed to. I learned it both in and out of school. MAHOGANY

You love school when it's interesting—and when it makes you feel smart. Getting good grades can make you feel that way. But also when you know the teachers care about you and your future: "I'm going to see you in five years, and you'll be in college." When they act like they think you'll be someone in life, not like you're dumb. VERONICA

Summary
HOW TO CREATE A CLASSROOM CULTURE OF SUCCESS

- Make clear your criteria for assessing our performance.

- Offer good models and help us see why they are good, not just their faults.

- Give helpful feedback and expect us to revise.

- Encourage our efforts even if we are having trouble.

- Remind us often that you expect our best.

- Give us plenty of support along the way.

- Help us set priorities among the different things we do.

- Don't favor the students you think will do the best.

- Don't compare us to other students.

CHAPTER 5

Teaching to the Individual, Working with the Group

"ONE JOB OF A TEACHER IS TO BE FAIR TO ALL.
DON'T EXPECT THE WORK OF ONE STUDENT FROM ANOTHER."

Teenagers don't like to be lumped together into a faceless crowd. As students make clear in Chapters 1 through 4, they want their teachers to know enough about them to accommodate, value, and respect their differences. At the same time they have a quick eye for the foibles of the adolescent character, and they appreciate the variety of student personalities teachers face in the classroom every day. One group of co-authors listed the following "types" that the typical classroom includes:

The eye-roller. Once angered or embarrassed by something, students like us stay that way throughout the course. We deliberately tune out, to make sure you get the message that we don't care.

The wallflower. Students like us may know the answer or have something to say, but we have a high level of anxiety about our ability to perform. We don't raise our hands, because we don't want to be noticed.

The hand-waver. Students like us need to prove to the teacher that we're knowledgeable or smart. Grades matter more than anything to us.

The dreamer. Students like us know plenty, but we don't have a drive to prove ourselves to teachers. We prefer to inhabit our own private world, which is usually more comfortable than the classroom.

The con artist. Students like us are always developing strategies to fool the teacher into thinking we know something. We're not necessarily cheaters, but we know how to play the game and win.

The goof-off. Students like us may be very smart, but to impress our peers we spend most of our time joking around and causing disruptions.

The workhorse. Students like us always come to class, do the homework, and answer the questions. We might not excel, but teachers can depend on us.

This mix occurs in any classroom, even in schools that sort students according to their academic backgrounds or ambitions. Kids' differences go on forever, as various as the cultures and families they come from. "Heterogeneous grouping," a practice that groups students of different achievement levels in the same classes, only represents yet one more form of variation a teacher can expect.

Given that every student has a unique profile of academics and personality, how can teachers pay attention to everyone's needs at once? How can they draw the eye-roller or the dreamer into class activities or discussions, while not letting the con artist or hand-waver dominate? When breaking the class into small groups, how can they arrange their very different students to maximize everyone's learning—not only of the subject material but also of important skills like collaboration, organization, and communication?

WHO PARTICIPATES, WHO DOESN'T, AND WHY

Many factors contribute to whether or not students speak up with their questions or contributions in class. They may not have confidence in the material, for example, or they may lack the skills to access it.

I had a friend who couldn't read, and I don't know how but she got through high school. She would make excuses when we read out loud in class—like, "I don't know what page we're at, can you go to the next person?" MAHOGANY

When I don't know the material, I don't even ask questions. I'm like, I might as well wait till the student next to me answers the question and I just fill it in. When I know the answer I would like to say it, and sometimes I raise my hand a little. But this one girl in my class always knows and the teacher goes to her automatically and calls on her instead. I don't want to be the one that's always shouting out the answer. LAURALIZ

Some students feel insecure about speaking in a way that opens them up to ridicule or makes them uncomfortable in other ways.

I don't want people to hear me talk because I don't want people to notice me. I have this fear that people judge me for every little thing. I stutter when I'm nervous, so it's a big thing for me, or I'll say a word wrong. LAURALIZ

If you push too hard, the student will sometimes feel threatened and just shut down. Or if you manage to push the student without upsetting him, and then he doesn't do it to your satisfaction, he might feel unworthy. ANDRES

If you show you know something, and raise your hand and know the answer, the teacher starts to treat you as like a crutch. Out of thirty-five kids, the teacher calls on someone and they don't answer. When finally someone raises their hand, the teacher feels relieved. VANCE

Students may simply feel disengaged from what's going on in class.

> The teacher talks with three kids in the class all the time, and everyone else is not doing anything. She thinks they're good discussions, but it's just the same three kids. BOSUNG

Or without intending it, teachers might be sending messages that students' questions are not opportunities for learning but rather annoying interruptions to the business of the class.

> I never liked chemistry or physics or anything, but one day I brought in a Stephen Hawking book on the history of the universe—I asked the teacher about it. He was talking about light, about how it's in packets, and how you can use light to turn chemicals into certain things. So I asked: "Couldn't you theoretically turn something into anything?" And he said: "No. That's science fiction," and went on with his class. And I'm thinking: "But Stephen Hawking said that—this is the only thing I have to contribute—I practiced all night to say this—" And so I just put my head back down on the desk. VANCE

> I have a teacher who shoots down questions because he thinks it's not an important question and he wants to continue on with the lesson. It's like he thinks I'm not very important. LAURALIZ

Students often develop strategies to fend off unwanted attention.

> I learned a technique so my teacher won't call on me: I look preoccupied with talking notes, or reading the pages being discussed. I'm like: Don't disturb me, I'm working on this right now. LAURALIZ

Or they may hold the floor with a lengthy but superficial answer aimed at "getting over," to create the impression they know more than they do.

> The more you talk the more they think you know. A friend of mine always raises his hand so that he looks like he knows—it's a bluff. VANCE

As students pointed out in Chapter 1, teachers can pick up signals about their kids' anxieties and needs by paying attention to the way they speak, act, and look.

> A teacher has to be mindful. Get to know your student, find out what are they feeling, why they're not answering questions today. They might be in a bad mood, or maybe someone said to them, "Shut the hell up." MIKA

> If a teacher sees a quiet person like me raise their hand, the teacher should call on that person right away. MONTOYA

When teachers pay this kind of attention, students gradually open up and participate more.

> It's a balancing act, like taking care of all your children. If a teacher takes the time to call on someone who doesn't always raise their hand, when the other student [who always contributes] raises their hand, the [quiet] student wouldn't feel so neglected. VANCE

DIFFERENT LEVELS IN ONE CLASS

Getting all kinds of students to open up in class creates an atmosphere where they can learn together even though they may have very different academic backgrounds. In fact, such differences become advantages, if the teacher treats everyone's perspective as valuable. If the opposite happens, students are quick to realize it.

We had tracking at my high school, different for every subject, five levels for math, three for science. Who was in which level was very segregated by race. It was a big school, and everyone just stayed in the level for all your classes. It wasn't based on your ability. HILARY

This one science teacher said: "If students are not doing well they should go back to eighth or seventh or sixth grade." That made me feel really bad, like he was separating the "smart" kids from the kids that were not doing so well. MONTOYA

Teachers sometimes fall into a pattern of asking questions that call for a brief, correct answer. Though students will usually feed back the required information, this technique doesn't help a classroom feel like a community. Depending on how they play the game of school, some kids will do only what it takes to get by without looking like a showoff. Others will do as little as possible without looking too dumb. By the way teachers ask and respond to questions, they can avoid putting students in either of these positions.

If they can't answer, ask another student, can anyone help them out? You generally feel more comfortable if one of your peers helps you, not the teacher. MARIBEL

Our Spanish teacher goes too fast. If someone asks a question, she turns to the person who is doing really well—maybe it's one of the Hispanic students—and she says, "But you understand, don't you?" and then she blows off the person who doesn't understand to look in the dictionary or ask somebody who knows. She's going to their level while we're still stuck on the last level. MONTOYA

I wish a teacher would ask me, "Do you understand? If not, how can I make you?" MAHOGANY

Kids learn more when teachers ask open-ended questions, then allow time for students to think something through together, gather evidence, and challenge the views of others. They find it harder but more interesting, and it gives more room for them to contribute at different levels.

A lot of times students don't answer because it's a question where you either get it right, or wrong. Instead, ask questions where there isn't a right or wrong answer. Ask students, "What's your opinion, what matters to you?" MIKA

Because of the difference of levels, it was a thing between the two groups—sometimes they'd be nervous, or try to rush and find the answer. But the teacher gave them equal chances. If they are embarrassed, depending on the class, the teacher can use an open-ended question that has no right or wrong answers. MARIBEL

If you give the student time, they will often figure it out themselves. But you can't wait forever, so if they don't give it, then take them out of the spotlight and help them out, guide them, give them some key words. TIFFANY

WORKING IN SMALL GROUPS

Talk isn't everything. Teachers who want to make sure that everyone in a diverse group really understands the material should set up purposeful group activities that depend on every student's *doing* things that foster learning. If the activity's end point demonstrates an actual grasp of important concepts, even learners with very different styles will have to show what they know. They won't be able to slide by with avoidance tactics, fast talk, or mere behavior compliance. And such activities also convey respect for a student's ability to figure things out and get something done.

> I like being able to do different activities because we all learn different. Some are visual and hands-on learners and others learn from books. So presentation and group work are great. And sometimes a student can explain it better to another student. MAHOGANY

> Small groups work in almost every subject. What I like about them is the independence—taking another route to the answer, other than what the teacher would recommend. Especially in math, everybody has their own routes to the answer. ANDRES

> The person who really doesn't know the material can learn from the person who does. LAURALIZ

Chapters 7 and 10 present more specific ideas for group activities and projects in various subject areas to engage students and develop deeper understanding. For now, we will concentrate on how the teacher can set up mixed groups so that every member must work hard, contribute, and learn. Students suggested the following guidelines:

Make sure the task contains challenges for everyone in the group.

> Sometimes they can be too easy, like making tessellations. If you're done you're just waiting there. Add an extra challenge, or think of something harder. ANDRES

Assign clear roles in the group. Let us use our particular areas of strength, but also stretch us to develop new ones. (See page 96.)

Design a group so there's a role for each kind of person. Like they can be the recorder of what everyone says. That's a start. They're still helping the group. They're still contributing. VANCE

Sometimes all quiet people can be good, but you have to be careful. [When we were teaching middle school kids in a summer program] we put all the dominant girls in one group together and they actually did the work. Then we put the quiet people all together and closed the door. We told them they only had this day to do it, and they had to do it. MARIBEL

Make sure we all pull our weight. As incentive, teachers can make participation part of the grade for a group activity, though that won't necessarily motivate every student.

You have to put the leech in with other people—they have to learn. If everyone has a particular job and you don't do that job, you don't get credit for it. LATIA

There's usually someone who doesn't care about doing well or is not affected if they don't get a good grade. DIANA

Don't let some of us dominate others.

I was in one group with a boyfriend and girlfriend who would dominate the conversation. That scares people from talking. TIFFANY

I guess we didn't mean to, but we kind of isolated the kid who couldn't speak Spanish because the three of us were talking Spanish so it would make it easier and not have to translate. ANDRES

Keep an eye on every group. Teachers should know how things are going in order to make changes, give advice, or keep the pressure on to get the work done.

> The teacher has to walk around and be attentive. LAURALIZ

> Don't leave the room! Stay around. LUIS

Let us sometimes pick what group to work in. This is especially important if we are expected to get together outside school hours.

> You may not get along with your assigned group, so the work isn't always done well. Letting you pick who you work with, or putting groups together that you know for sure will work, is good. DIANA

> I don't learn in group projects because usually there's one person who does the whole thing while other people are talking. She does assign people to groups, but she doesn't know the students! If she knew them she would know who to assign me with—she should put the people who know a lot already with people who wouldn't take advantage of them. LAURALIZ

Students with widely different characteristics and backgrounds can learn a lot in small group work—but only if the teacher takes advantage of their differences in setting up the work. Some ways to achieve this:

Have a meaningful product the group will create.
Whether it's a paper, a presentation, a boat, or a bridge, the product should take all kinds of talents to carry off well. (For example, building a bridge could involve skills in art, computers, construction, leadership, organization, and so forth.)

Know what makes a team.
Get the class to describe the roles that contribute to a successful team (such as leader, recorder, computer person, organizer-scheduler-manager, artist, observer-critiquer). Then have students identify their own styles in group work (using a process such as the one on page 96). Finally, ask students to help develop a rubric that spells out responsibilities for each role.

Give everyone in the group a specific role.
In their first try at group work, students should be given a role in which they already have talent. Then, in successive group activities and projects, assign students roles that stretch them just enough to create a challenge. Give them coaching and support (from expert students or appropriate adults) in how to do a role that's new or difficult for them. Ask them to reflect on their new roles in journals or discussions, to help them appreciate the different strengths individuals bring to a group project.

Assess individual performance and final product separately.
Students should get an individual assessment of how each carried out the assigned role. In addition, the final product should receive a grade or assessment that all group members share.

IDENTIFYING INDIVIDUAL ROLES FOR SMALL GROUP WORK

Is a student a natural leader in a group? An obvious choice for the group's computer expert? More of a note-taker or a worker bee? The following exercise can help students lead the way in identifying the roles for successful group work.

1. Randomly divide the class into sets of four or five and ask students to develop a list of the roles that someone in any group must fill to do any project together. (*Examples:* chairperson, recorder, artist, computer expert, scheduler, spokesperson, fact checker, researcher.)

2. After all groups have a list, share them with the whole class. What are their similarities? What are their differences? Together, come up with a short list of roles necessary for any group task.

3. Then ask students to take each role on the list and briefly describe what kind of person would do it well. (*Examples:* Leader = good listener, organized, inspiring, and so forth; recorder = fast writer, good speller, organized, clear note-taker, and so on. Worker = follows instructions well, attention to detail, motivated, and so on.)

4. Again, share these with the whole class. The teacher or students can boil them down into a rubric for each role, which can then be posted on the board or typed up to use the next day.

5. Finally, ask each student to answer these questions:

- Which role are you currently best suited for? What evidence do you have for that in your previous experiences?
- Which role are you currently least suited for? What evidence do you have for that in your previous experiences?
- How might you change that by learning from what others do?
- What other roles do you think you could do well, and why?

Students will then be ready to start working on an actual project. They all should know what strengths they bring to the group task, and what weaknesses they need to work on to be a more effective team player. At the end of the project, use the rubrics the class developed to assess how well each student performed as a member of the group.

PROGRESS IS INDIVIDUAL

Just as a group of students may come to understanding via different paths, they also make progress on different timetables. As long as they are trying hard to meet a worthy standard, kids want the teacher to respect and support these individual paces.

> My best teacher have patience with his students. He won't rush anyone. Some teachers will tell you to hurry up and do your work, and then it be messy and they give you a bad grade on it. PORSCHE

> In ninth grade, when I was trying to get out of the slump I was in, the teacher at the end of the term saw me working more. And he erased some of the days—it allowed me to get caught up. ANDRES

It's also important to remember that every student in a class will not be able to produce work of the same quality. The teacher should look for progress, not necessarily uniformity of product—at the same time emphasizing the habits of revision and diligence that eventually make excellent work possible for everyone.

> Don't expect the work of one student from another. Last year we had people that barely spoke English in our literature class. There are a lot of students in a class with different learning levels. One job of a teacher is to be fair to all. ANDRES

> It's really important the teachers know their students as individuals. You need to know, not to lower your expectations but to be realistic. HILARY

Keep in close enough touch with students to know when and why they need an extension. If a student needs more time to turn in a paper that meets high expectations of quality, it doesn't necessarily mean the student has learned less.

CAN STANDARDS BE AS INDIVIDUAL AS STUDENTS?

Students know that the world respects people who meet high standards for a task—whether that means playing basketball or writing a book. But they also know that high school kids can't typically play at the NBA level and that high school writers are rarely published. So when teachers assess students using standards, they need to remember several things:

Spell out what you're looking for in the assignment.
We need to know more than the required length and due date. What qualities will you assess in our final product (content knowledge, originality or creativity, use of evidence, organization, style or presentation, mechanics)? Will you also be assessing our process (collaboration, timing, revision)? How much will each element count?

Give examples of what work looks like at different levels.
Just like people, good work doesn't all look the same. Use class time to show us how a piece of work might be strong on ideas and weak on mechanics, or strong on presentation but weaker on supporting evidence. Let us talk about how we would assess work that has both strong and weak qualities.

Use a rubric to assess our work.
Spell out expectations in a clear checklist that breaks down into matters of content, organization, mechanics, presentation, and process. Don't just count up points, but give us feedback on why we did well and how to improve.

Give us the chance to revise.
Almost nobody can meet high standards without going back and revising work after feedback. If you care about high quality, build revision into every important assignment, even if you have to cover less content by doing so.

The complex issue of honoring individual progress in a diverse group is one of a new teacher's most fundamental challenges—and thus goes hand in hand with many other subjects this book addresses in other chapters: knowing students well (Chapter 1), treating them fairly (Chapter 2), conveying high expectations (Chapter 4), creating motivation (Chapter 6), teaching difficult material (Chapter 7), and teaching students whose English-language skills are just developing (Chapter 8). With their passion for justice, students can act as important arbiters in the process of figuring out what's fair. Their most important message: Don't forget to ask us!

Summary
THE INDIVIDUAL AND THE GROUP

- Recognize why we participate and why we might not.

- Take advantage of our differences.

- Ask open-ended questions that invite individual perspectives.

- Make sure the task contains challenges for everyone in the group.

- Assign clear roles in the group.

- Make sure we all pull our weight.

- Don't let some of us dominate others.

- Keep an eye on every group.

- Let us sometimes pick what group to work in.

CHAPTER 6

Motivation and Boredom

"JUST SAYING YOU NEED TO PASS MATH ISN'T ENOUGH.
SHOW ME HOW KNOWING PI IS WORTH SOMETHING."

Our society makes most teenagers go to school. Just at the point in life when kids want more than anything to make their own choices, they must accept that fact, at least until the age dictated by law.

> School is like a chapter in your life. You have your baby chapter when you don't do anything, and then the K–12 chapter, where you learn basic things—history, math, holidays. Then you tell society you've moved on through that stage, so you're ready to go on into the adult world. ALEXIS

Assuming they do comply and show up, adolescents face another blow to their sense of autonomy: They typically get little say in how their schools and classes function.

> I felt like school was keeping me from learning. I wanted to read books I chose and do my own art, but you didn't have time. HILARY

> School felt like a prison in eighth and ninth grades. My mom leaves for work before I get up in the morning, and I saw no reason to attend. I had no motivation. I was suffocated. ANDRES

Is it any wonder that so many teenagers do not respond with eagerness and energy to the work of school? The miracle, in fact, is that so many do.

KIDS KNOW SCHOOL IS IMPORTANT

Even though students may resent being compelled to go to school or might wish school were different, they accept that school is an important route to independence.

> School is my way out, into taking care of myself. I can't see myself living in my grandmother's house any longer, depending on them. Also, I really want the college experience. My mom says the college years are the best of your life, and school is the way to get there. But out of six of my classes, three are interesting and three are a waste of time. MAHOGANY

> I know I'm not going to get anywhere without it. It's also a way to get out of the house. I think if school were a choice, some people would actually show up—and not just the straight-A students. There's only so much to do outside school. DIANA

> If you want to stay in your realm, you can't blame the man if you don't get ahead. The opportunities are there, even though you have to bust your ass. It's not that it's easy for everybody. It's like a slave who learns how to read and own their own newspaper in slave times. ALEXIS

They realize school offers opportunities for growth, both academic and social.

> I go to school because I like to learn new things, new ways. There are some classes that I don't like, but I will take them anyway just to move on and reach my full potential. ANDRES

> You need to go to learn how to cooperate, to work with people that you don't know, to trust in people. You have drama at school—people getting in conflicts with each other and everything—so you learn who you can trust of your peers and your teachers. DIANA

And they appreciate the chance to be around adults who care about them.

> School lets you find some adults you can connect with. There's stuff that you have to talk to adults about, that you can't talk to your parents about, maybe something really important like pregnancy that you know you have to take care of. ANDRES

Student co-authors listed their own reasons for being in school:

> To ward off ignorance.
>
> To teach others.
>
> To be social.
>
> To see others' points of view.
>
> To understand history so history isn't repeated.
>
> To become well rounded.
>
> To be well represented; to have a voice.
>
> To learn to survive in society.
>
> To find a career path and a well-paying job.
>
> To know information so you're not stuck in "duh" stages, even if things may not seem useful now.
>
> Well, what else are you gonna do in the day that's productive?

Then they offered their opinions on why society makes them attend, whether they want to or not:

> So we won't be out on the streets, doing crime, being in gangs. Also, they don't want the next generations to be totally uneducated. They need someone to take control, to keep going on with technology and all. You can't have uneducated people running Microsoft. DIANA

So what they tell you will become part of what you're thinking. Same as when they told black people they were meant to be slaves or entertainers, and that's what they grew up thinking. I hate school when the information that I'm learning doesn't reflect the person that I am. TIFFANY

It gives them a way to have control over what you do. In school a lot of what they do is keep control over what you do—nitpicky stuff like which classes you're allowed to take without certain requirements, that's one of the things I really hate. HILARY

Even though the city officials say it's about learning and preparing people for their future, it's about more than academics. What you need to succeed in society shifts: thirty years ago you didn't need computers. Now the goal may be different but you're still going somewhere. Just the fact that you did it—that's what people respect. You took a journey and you completed it. It's a rite of passage into adulthood. VANCE

WHAT MOTIVATES KIDS?

Although teenagers know and usually accept why they're in school, the actual experience can either grind them down into boredom and resistance or build their interest in what they do there. The extent to which they feel motivated depends on several key factors:

Passionate teachers. A teacher who cares about both the material and the students has an enormous effect on how much students care about learning.

The mark of a good teacher is that no matter how weird or boring you might think their subject is, their love for it is what pushes you to learn something. It could be rat feces or some nasty topic, and the fact that their eyes are glowing when they talk about it makes you want to know something about it. VANCE

If they have a passion for teaching kids, it's much easier for them to teach, period. I don't think most teachers have a passion, and you can tell if they do. MAHOGANY

Conversely, students easily spot—and respond in kind to—apathetic teachers.

Some teachers act like they don't want to be there. They don't have any spirit, they just make the class do work. Once in a while students want to laugh and have fun. MONTOYA

[One teacher I had] acted like she didn't want to be at school, like she was in another world. She don't play games or show any movies to help us learn, to make it fun. She don't ask if anybody knows what they're doing. She just give us a quiz and expect us to pass it. PORSCHE

Issues kids care about. Teenagers are constantly seeking answers to some of life's most important questions. They want to spend their mental energy on things that matter to them.

When we were reading James Baldwin we did a Socratic seminar about the role that religion played in the decisions the characters made. One question was, "Do you think religion is a positive influence in society?" Usually when I'm sleeping, I wake up with an idea and have a pencil by my bed, and after that I had a lot of ideas on this; it really made me think. When we had to construct the essay, I read through all my little notes from when I woke up. I already had the answer, and he found the right question to ask. ANDRES

If every day teachers would ask me things that I would be interested in, I would have a different feeling about school. I might like school if it was about animals. I want to be a vet or work with animals. I would do the other work for that. DIANA

The books you read, the movies you see don't all have to be about white people fighting each other! PORSCHE

Connections to the real world. Just teaching "by the book" bores anybody, not only teenagers. Student interest increases when teachers find ways to bring the material alive.

We had to read *Night* by Elie Wiesel, and my teacher found someone who was in a prison camp. She was pretty old and she remembers most of it and told us a few stories. It made us realize how real it was that people actually went to prison camp. ANDRES

My English teacher taught so many things about words and also life. She inspired me to keep on writing my poetry and writing stories about my feelings. PORSCHE

My math teacher kept trying to connect to me using formulas and problems and to be honest, I don't care enough about math to respond. Maybe it's wrong, but I need something personal to motivate me. If he could connect geometry angles to my interest in art or being an actor, that would work. Just saying you need to pass math to get out of high school isn't enough. Show me how knowing pi is worth something. VANCE

In biology class I have learned things I never heard about: biology and life, sexual viruses, things like that. It was important because you got to learn about what kind of diseases would happen if you didn't take care about yourself when having sexual relationships. That teacher changed my life. VERONICA

Choices on things that matter. The more students have a voice in important decisions about how and what they learn, the more involved and motivated they feel.

We don't want the teachers to be in control, we want to be more involved. LUIS

When we get to choose what to read or what to write about, it's easier to get interested in something. LAURALIZ

HELPING KIDS STAY MOTIVATED

Curriculum that engages students' interest isn't the only way to keep them motivated. Little things in how a teacher conducts the class or responds to students also make a big difference. Student co-authors gave these examples:

Make learning a social thing.

When I know everybody in a classroom, I feel comfortable to talk, because I know they won't laugh at me. At my old high school, which was big, I almost never knew most people in my classes. At my new high school, a small one, I know everyone. PORSCHE

My best teacher always has us up and doing experiments to make it fun, working in groups, playing games. That's how he gets us to learn. PORSCHE

It can be fun to do activities and group work, because you get to talk but also learn with your friends. Some people's attention span is very short, so listening to the teacher is stressful and they get distracted. DIANA

We were learning about the British Isles in global studies, and when I was talking to this girl, I noticed she had an accent. I was like, "Are you from Britain?" It turned out she was South African, which was colonized by the English, and then I learned that my teacher from India was also from a colony. So I not only learned some history, but also I learned not to categorize people by their accents. VANCE

Make sure we understand.

Sometimes I won't do the work because I don't understand what's going on. If I tell my math teacher "I don't understand" she's like, "Whatever, do it anyway"—so then I'm not interested in working, and I blow her off and don't do it. DIANA

I used to be that person that knows the material—now I'm not so much because the material is harder and I don't like the teacher. They're losing me. I'm not learning when I should be learning. LAURALIZ

When we don't pay attention because we're bored, we don't understand. MONTOYA

Respond with interest when we show interest.

I like when you ask them a question and they don't give you a direct answer. They ask, "What do you think? What if that were true? What's the evidence?" LATIA

I had a teacher once and when a student asked a question off the subject, she said, "We'll talk about that another time." She was a really traditional teacher and we didn't think she would. But the next day she came in and had a whole class planned around that question. I thought it was great. She listened and she adapted what she did to that. LATIA

Care about us and our progress.

I wouldn't even think I could do something and my teacher would push me farther and I would succeed and do really well. In those first two months we did tons of work, and at the end we had a big project to do. I couldn't believe all the work I did. MONTOYA

It's all about coaxing. Sometimes I'll come home and not feel like doing anything, yet I'll literally force myself to, purely out of predilection for the teacher. LATIA

Help us keep on top of our workload.

I hate school when I have a lot of work piled up, which is almost always. I have a hard time concentrating on what I'm doing at home; I'll get up and go watch TV, or I'll be sleeping. If all my work took place in school, I would be fine. I stay after school sometimes and do my work at school. DIANA

In seventh grade my grades started slipping. I noticed I had a lot more freedom, and I stopped doing my work. But they kept on passing me, even though I wasn't doing anything. It's not like it was about my learning, it was about moving us through to high school. I hated that. ANDRES

Show your pride in our good work.

> I think you could make [kids care more] by feeling happy about and connected to your class. Act like you're proud of them, like "that's my student!"
> VERONICA

> Sometimes I can't wait to get up and go to school. Because at some points school is very interesting—like when we have exhibition night, where everybody shows their projects off. MONTOYA

> At my eighth-grade graduation I was so proud of myself. I worked hard for three years and I was so happy I graduated. PORSCHE

Provide role models to inspire us.

> Nothing motivates me more than seeing successful people and having it not be a mystery how they got successful. Some teachers will bring in an actor, a writer, a history buff, a political activist—they don't know anything about teaching, but they connect to the students and they can help us. Teenagers don't see the future—it's hazy. You think you're going to live forever. At that point teachers need to show us how doing things now builds the steps that pay off in the future, in our twenties. VANCE

> Teachers should instill in students that what you do now really affects what happens to you later—it can either break you or make your life easier. If you just do your work for four years, you can have a choice as to what college you go to, and get to do what you want to do. They should break down life in the beginning, not at the end—maybe bring people in, talk about famous or successful people who had rough starts. People need to visualize it. ALEXIS

TIMING IS EVERYTHING

School doesn't give students—or teachers—much say in when they do things. The daily schedule typically sets limits on what's possible in a given class period, and the school calendar imposes a certain urgency about what students must accomplish by year's end. Add to this a host of requirements, including standardized tests and college applications, and school can feel almost military in its regimentation.

But when teachers modify the timing of those requirements, students benefit. In fact, because teenagers have different biological rhythms from those of adults, scheduling their schoolwork thoughtfully can greatly influence both their motivation and their performance.

For example, since adolescents have a natural need to sleep later in the morning, they rarely feel alert and active in the first class period of the day. By second period they can handle just about anything, they acknowledge. But toward lunchtime, their willingness to work declines as they get hungrier. After lunch, some feel energized, others want to take it slow. And nobody wants to do unappetizing things, like dissections, either before or after eating.

Vacations, school dances and other exciting events, or even great weather also reduce students' motivation to pay attention to homework, projects, tests, and other schoolwork.

> Right before a vacation is definitely not a good time for a test. You're so close to vacation, and you don't feel like trying; you rationalize it that it's okay, and really you're going to feel bad about it later. You should have the test the week before, or a week after the vacation—not immediately after. Let them get back into the groove and recap what they need to know. BOSUNG

It's almost impossible to get everyone to agree on a good time for difficult or demanding work. Students have a natural tendency to delay or resist it, and teachers have an obligation to make it happen. But kids' motivation increases when teachers have asked these questions before planning an activity:

- Does the timing of this task conflict with the physical needs of students?

- Does the timing of the task conflict with another important priority for students, either in or outside school?

- Have students had enough preparation time and advance support to do this task well?

- Have students had the chance to give input on when the activity will happen?

Though they didn't always agree on every detail, student co-authors put together the chart on page 111 to offer some suggestions on timing activities at different times of the day and the year. Any teacher could try making a similar chart as a classroom exercise at the beginning of the term. Talking with students about the best times for various activities can give them practice in balancing the requirements of the school day and year with the needs of different people involved, and increase their sense of ownership in the schedule. (Some schools put up a big calendar marking test days or project days; in one huge suburban school, each department even has a specified "test day.")

WHEN SHOULD WE DO THAT? A Planning Chart by Students

Time of day or year	A good time to...	A bad time to...
First week of school	Give a quick quiz to see what students know Get to know students Tell students about you Make rules with students Introduce the semester	Joke around; be too nice Judge; yell Assign homework (you're just getting used to school after summer)
First thing in the morning	Have something active to wake people up Discuss, not write	Give a big test Give a lecture Have gym
Before lunch	Give a lecture about something important Do a fun activity, an educational movie, or an outdoor project Have gym Read and write	Do activities that deal with food (makes you hungry) Talk about disgusting stuff Have major projects Give a test Have a long talk with a hungry student
After lunch	Write Give a test Exercise, have fun, play games before working	Give a lecture Do physical activities (disagreement on this) Do nasty projects like dissection
Last period	Have discussions Watch a serious movie Do some group work Have recreation or gym	Have a test (not focused, ready to go home) Give a load of homework (other classes have already given it) Give a speech or lecture
Beautiful day	Have class outside Do something educational in the park Read or do activities outside	Send students out alone Stay in and watch a movie Stay in the classroom Read from a dull textbook
Day before a holiday break	Have a makeup day Write about different things students are doing Have a party	Give a major test Start a new subject or project Give homework
Day after a holiday break	Review previous work and get into new subject Talk or write about vacation	Give a test or quiz Have homework due Give a big project
College application deadline week	Give time in school to help with applications	Assign a lot of homework Give tests
During standardized tests	Do quick prep reviews using games or old work Bring snacks	Give homework or projects Give other tests
Senior spring	Do free reading or writing Do a senior project	Introduce new topics Give a lot of work
Last week of school	Have parties and trips Have performances, presentations, project exhibitions Evaluate the course	Give hard, new, serious work Have an important test

HOMEWORK AND ITS DISCONTENTS

Homework certainly qualifies as one of the least popular aspects of school. If students take five classes a day, they usually go home with work to do in at least half of them, and if they have after-school activities or jobs, the time spent on homework can be a real burden. When homework clearly forms the basis for the next day's class, kids can buy into it. Otherwise, they often don't see the point.

> Homework, if it's given right, can help you learn more. But, depending on the class, it's not always necessary. DIANA

> Summer school doesn't assign homework. ANDRES

> You usually don't get a lot out of homework. It seems like a regulatory kind of thing. You're not supposed to think about it, you're just supposed to do it and turn it in the next day. We get packets in history with the dates all highlighted; you take the dates and you answer the questions. I don't remember any of them. If they didn't give it, it would be a lot more fun and you would learn as much. It would be better to have an extra hour of school. ANDRES

Some of the reasons students give for not doing their homework:

> There's too much in each subject, so something has to go.

> There's no time, given all our other commitments (sports, clubs, work, family responsibilities, and so forth).

> The teacher never checks the homework anyway.

> Doing the homework isn't necessary for full participation in the class.

HOW TO MAKE HOMEWORK MATTER TO US

Do...	Don't...

Use homework to prepare for important activities. If a big exam is coming up, give out a study checklist. If you're having a Socratic seminar or a role-play the next day, give the reading we will need to have done.

Give homework that uses resources that exist at home but not at school, like interviewing an elderly person about the Depression era.

Take class time for some typical homework activities. Sustained silent reading or writing in class helps everyone keep up with important preparation.

Cooperate with other teachers. Know what we are getting for homework in other classes, and design your own assignments not to compete. Go easy on homework when we have something big due in another subject. Try to assign homework that can actually tie in or help out with work in other classes.

Make it matter. Give points when we do our homework. Even if something is wrong, give credit if we have tried.

Turn it into learning. If a student is having trouble with the homework, take time to explain. Take it as a signal that someone needs extra help.

Use homework as creative time. Ask us to brainstorm ways to solve a problem you haven't yet addressed in class. (For example: Design a paper airplane that flies in a loop, and try to explain why it works.)

Provide a supportive setting (like a study session in a quiet classroom with a tutor on hand) where we can do the work at school if home isn't a good place.

Load it on. We can reasonably handle a total of only two to three hours a night of homework, and for students with other responsibilities, that's probably too much. Try doing your own homework assignment to see how long it takes you. Then double that time—at least—to estimate how long it will take someone who's just learning.

Use it for trivial activities. Some assignments don't fulfill any important function and are just asking for us to copy each other's homework. Better to eliminate that kind of homework altogether.

Use it to introduce a new skill that requires support. That kind of work should take place in class.

Blame students without investigating. When someone hasn't done the homework, don't jump to conclusions. Find out if there's something they didn't understand. If someone makes mistakes on homework, take it as an occasion to see where the student needs more support.

Give homework over vacation, for the most part. Aside from certain exceptions to keep up important habits—like reading a book, or watching a television show in the foreign language we are studying—it's not fair to have to spend a vacation that way. We do appreciate knowing about a big assignment coming up after the break that we could get a head start on. But don't require it to be ready immediately after vacation.

The homework is trivial and boring.

The homework is too hard, so we give up.

We don't have a quiet place to do it, or anyone to ask for help with it.

We sit still and work all day in school; why should we have to do it at home, too?

If teachers want to increase kids' motivation to do homework, they should make sure the homework really matters, tell students exactly why, and follow up on it reliably. On page 114, student co-authors list for teachers their Do's and Don'ts about homework.

READING AND WRITING: WHERE MOTIVATION COUNTS MOST

Kids learn more in every academic area when they are highly motivated to read and write, so it's definitely worth a teacher's time in any subject to help students take pleasure in doing these things. What approaches work best to encourage teenagers' interest in reading and writing? Students offered these suggestions:

Know what we already like to read and write. No matter what subject you're teaching, start every new term by finding out what kinds of things we already read or write—just because we want to. Post a list of our choices so we can add to it and you can refer to it throughout the term. You'll probably see some ways to link what we care about to the things you want us to learn in class.

> At home I read the *Oakland Tribune* and sometimes websites for music or video games. They make me write about the newspaper, a summary of what I read, then we discuss it in class. LUIS

On my own time I like to read urban novels, and about civil disobedience. MAHOGANY

When I'm mad I read song lyrics. DIANA

Give us choices about what we read and write. Wherever you can, let us choose our reading and the topics we write about. Don't worry if it's something you wouldn't care about yourself. People can learn the power of reading and writing from anything.

> At first we had an outside reading program where you picked your own book and did a movie poster or an essay about it. People did it, but then they changed it and gave you a list of things you had to read. Now nobody does it anymore. MAHOGANY

> We had to choose someone who was famous or had done something interesting and write a paper about them. I really wanted to write about Eminem, so I got all my info on him and looked for anything else I could find on the computer. After all that, my teacher told me what I had wasn't enough or good enough to write a whole paper, so I had to do someone else, and the paper ended up really bad. I don't think any of my teachers like Eminem, and they didn't want me to write about him. DIANA

Ask us to share our reactions to what we read and write. Help us think of print as another way of talking back and forth about ourselves and our lives. Everybody sees written-down things in different ways depending on our own life experiences, and we can learn from each other. Treat all our responses as important, whether or not we like something or agree with the experts.

> It makes me feel uncomfortable when books don't reflect the person that

I am, when we're always reading things by white males, not by any African American or Asian or Hispanic people. TIFFANY

In an essay we had to write on the U.S. Constitution, I took a position no one in my class, including my teacher, agreed with. It was very pressurizing, yet extremely motivating. LATIA

Our teacher told us to make our own island and we had to decide how we were going to survive, what we were going to do, what was our government, who was going to be in control. He was in a corner, and he was writing things down about how we reacted to the situation of him not being in control. It connected to *Lord of the Flies*, and that's why we read Hobbes. For homework we had to write about how we felt being in control and how we felt when he ignored us. MONTOYA

Bring drama and creative art into our reading and writing life. Some of us don't get the world of print as easily as others, especially if we are working in a new language. (If you've ever learned a foreign language you might remember that at first it's easier to read comic books than regular books!) If we can act out or draw something, we can often imagine and respond to it more deeply, calling on our past experiences and learning to take different perspectives, too. Talking together about our artistic responses is fun, and it can lead us to take new risks in reading and writing.

My teacher knows that some books are boring, so she compares them to our lives. Or we make a play and act it out. Or we pick one person—we have to pretend it's us and tell the class about us. MAHOGANY

We had to make a ten-minute play about if Antony and Cleopatra were in these days. It was the ghetto version, Tamika and Pookey. I was Tamika.

There were seven scenes. We had them die in a car accident. They went back in time and we got a scene from the real *Antony and Cleopatra* and put it in there. PORSCHE

Treat writing and reading as windows into our lives. We can use them to come to terms with the things that matter most to us—our families and friends, our struggles, our emotional issues. If you want us to care about reading and writing, relate it whenever possible to ourselves and those we care about.

When I was a little girl I used to make up stories and write them down. My family is always telling me I should write down the story of my family because—whew!—it's a story to tell! I tried to, but it's so complicated. And I would like to get some more history on my mother—my mother has medical problems and she lives two buildings away. She's had three husbands, and I live with my aunt and my little brother. But I want to have a degree first, and do something with my life, and then write this book so people will pay attention. So in some ways—someday—I want to make that piece of writing the best it can possibly be. But now I'm more insecure—I always have to look up words in the dictionary. In school, I don't write. I'm passing with a 90, but my teacher isn't having us write anything. LAURALIZ

When I try to express how I feel about some situations, I write the best I can, so people can see the anger inside me or the happiness or sadness I have in my heart. Sometimes I work over that writing again and again. VERONICA

Give us some time in school for required reading. Not everyone has enough time and quiet to read outside school.

> Reading goes good in school. Every day in the morning my teacher assigns 30 minutes of class time to read, so everyone can be caught up with what we are reading. We have five questions to fill out with things like character information. Also, on one day every week my advisory is extra long, and for 40 minutes we just read anything we want. ANDRES

> During the first 20 minutes of our second class we have "sustained silent reading." Sometimes we go longer. MAHOGANY

Get us in the habit of free writing. For a few minutes several times a week, ask us to write short informal responses in class to anything that relates to the subject. (For example, we could write about our thoughts on controversial issues in science, our opinion about how public opinion polls can manipulate statistics, our response to a movie or a TV show, how we might feel if we found ourselves in situations from books or the news.) This helps us see writing as an extension of ourselves and a way to think things through, rather than thinking of it as answering somebody else's questions correctly. Treat what we write as important, by responding to it or sharing it (if it's not too private).

> I wanted to write a poem in my English class after I saw that movie *American History X*. It was so sad that I just had to write about it because it really made me think bad things, so I had to write it down instead of saying something to someone. PORSCHE

> When we were reading this book called *Night* there were things I wanted to write about—when it said that people would throw the little babies into the air and shoot them, and kill people and burn them. It made me

so mad and I wanted to write bad things about people. Nobody had asked me to write about it, but I did, in my Dear Diary book. Ooh, if I was right there I would have just done something. VERONICA

I always want to write down ideas, thoughts, or just interesting facts that I notice while walking or thinking to myself. The problem is I usually don't have paper or a pen and I usually don't remember what I was thinking. But when I do, I can write for pages and pages about something I think is wrong, or don't like, or think should change, looking at it from all angles. ANDRES

Show us our writing matters by having us revise and publish it. If you care enough to make it public, we care more about what we say and how we say it.

I wrote this poem about this fifteen-year-old girl getting pregnant. I just had to make it the best, because there is so many young girls getting pregnant at a young age that I know people would want to read it. PORSCHE

I hate writing assignments for school. Essays are a true heckle. Sometimes I get the urge to write a novel, though. In fact, my plan is to start one this summer. There's a rush, I'm not getting any younger. The teenage writer factor is fast expiring. LATIA

Getting published is a big motivator. The people who publish the *Muzine* [a local literary magazine] come to our class and pick out the best to publish. I kept working on the same poem so many times it wasn't even funny, and they have chosen to put it in. SANDY

WHAT WE READ WHEN WE CAN CHOOSE

Lauraliz
The newspaper
Seventeen magazine
Romance books

Mika
All the poetry I can get
 my hands on
Trashy romance novels
Cosmopolitan (funny
 stories)
"Political" books (books
 with message)
Sista Souljah—No
 Disrespect
Plays—published and
 unpublished
Unpublished pieces from
 independent authors
Lyrics

Vance
Comic books
Entertainment Weekly
Internet message boards
Maxim
Video game books and
 magazines
Art books
Easy Rawlins mysteries
Sci-fi
Articles
Poetry
Essence

Latia
Watchtowers and *Awakes*
 that come in the mail
The Bible
The New York Times
The Village Voice
*Time Magazine, Teen
 People, Essence, Honey,
 Slam, YM, Cosmogirl,*
 and any other magazine
 I can find
*A Separate Peace, Flyy Girl,
 The Fountainhead*

Veronica
Oakland Tribune
 (Bay Area Living and the
 front page)
Books
Hip hop and teen magazines
Poems that my friends
 write
Kids' stories, like "Snow
 White," to my little sisters
Driver's permit manual
Autobiographies—I like all
 of them
Books my aunt gave me
 about inventions
 (because she knows I
 like inventing things,
 like a cage for birds)

Porsche
My poems I write
Nickelodeon, Essence, Vibe,
 teen magazines
Oakland Tribune (the
 weather, horoscope,
 cartoons sometimes)
Bus schedules
Ingredients on food labels
When my brothers and
 sisters want me to read
 to them, *The Cat in
 the Hat* is my favorite
 book—hecka rhymes!
When my teachers assign
 a book (*Night*)

Montoya
Oakland Tribune
 (horoscopes, cartoons,
 front page)
Cookbooks (I've been
 cooking since age twelve,
 I like to do that)
Teen magazines
Avon—we all get a lot
Directions and maps
Comic books (Snoopy,
 coffee break section)

Andres
The newspaper
Magazines about video
 games, computers,
 bicycling, anime
Advertisements
Books (for school, graphic
 novels, chapter books)
Comic books

Summary

HOW TO GET AND KEEP KIDS MOTIVATED

- Be passionate about your material and your work.

- Connect to issues we care about outside school.

- Give us choices on things that matter.

- Make learning a social thing.

- Make sure we understand.

- Respond with interest when we show interest.

- Care about us and our progress.

- Help us keep on top of our workload.

- Show your pride in our good work.

- Provide role models to inspire us.

CHAPTER 7

Teaching Difficult Academic Material

"SHE SNATCHES HISTORY FROM THE PAST AND PUTS IT IN MY BACKYARD."

A teacher's efforts to know students well and create a culture of mutually respectful expectations really start to pay off when a class works on difficult academic material. All that effort builds a partnership between teacher and class, in which kids trust that they have something to gain from paying attention, doing the work, and playing by the rules. The teacher shows competence and interest in the subject, and teaches in ways that recognize students' individual needs. Students get used to working together, even if they bring different levels of prior knowledge or various personal qualities to the task. Kids develop the habits of readers and writers, while the teacher grows increasingly adept at listening and responding to their opinions.

If all this is happening, the engine of the classroom has its working parts ready for something hard, perhaps material with especially high stakes. If the teacher merely presents that material as information students must receive and spit back, learning it will probably feel about as motivating as root canal work— and it won't last.

> You just had it memorized, you really didn't learn it. DIANA

> Lots of teachers will give you every step leading up to the answer. You're not really learning anything, you're just reciting it. VANCE

But if the teacher supports teenagers in proving their strength, ability, and independence through demanding intellectual action, kids can experience the adventure and excitement of an expedition into new territory.

In this chapter, students describe tactics that help them approach difficult material, no matter what the subject. Then they comment on teaching techniques that have worked well for them as they tackled hard work in specific subject areas: math and science, literature, and history.

GETTING KIDS GOING

Learning hard things feels most overwhelming when students see the new material as a daunting mass of unfamiliar ideas. But students say a teacher can help break through that barrier by trying things like this:

Find out what we know already.

> Everyone knows things in history at least superficially—everyone's heard the term "Industrial Revolution." I had a teacher who on the first day said: What happened in the American Revolution? the Civil War? and so on. That can tell you so much. MIKA

> Sometimes teachers think they're the first one to teach you something. They don't realize that we might have been listening for five years to someone else that wasn't you. VANCE

> But sometimes you don't remember—you need that little spark to remind you. So don't judge them from their answers on the first kid [they ask]. LAURALIZ

Link hard material to what we already know.

> My teacher can make Hawaii into "Bell Atlantic" and the U.S. into "AT&T" and explain Hawaii's annex in two seconds flat. She snatches history from the past and puts it in my backyard. LATIA

My history teacher connects many things with things today. There's this thing with Tariff Union that I think Germany did, and he's relating it to what Europe is doing now with euros, how they traded without tax and tariffs. That catches us. MARIBEL

Break down complicated material.

Especially with hard subjects, it's difficult to figure out what they're trying to teach if you don't know it yet. For chemistry they gave us a really difficult book to read; it used words that I didn't have any idea of. It was a really good book, I could tell, but I didn't have any incentive to read it. I couldn't concentrate, because the assumptions were that you knew a lot already. BOSUNG

My math teacher goes as slow as necessary—gives examples, tells stories, makes assignments and handouts to clear up questions. We do charts, and blind guessing. You can't stop until you get it. MIKA

Try different ways to approach things.

If students don't understand, [good teachers find] other ways to explain it. Like if a teacher is telling you how to do something in math, someone might be a visual thinker and need to try a diagram on the board. BOSUNG

You pay attention if the people you are identified with are represented. All my life I have been studying what Europeans and Americans do, but not Africans. So when we studied the Cold War, she gave us an article from an African textbook and we saw how differently they learn about it there. It gave us a sense of how different [studying history] could be. TIFFANY

Make connections among the things we're learning.

> In my humanities class, when we did a certain assignment or project, it would connect to the next thing we would study, or the next assignment. It made it very easy for me to learn. MONTOYA

PUSHING STUDENTS' THINKING

Once teachers have a sense of what students already think or know, they can push into new territory. Making the classroom a place where students and teachers alike test each other's thinking is particularly effective. Students suggest several ways to do that:

Ask questions that really make us think.

> I was sitting in history really bored, and I was wondering how could history help me? And he could tell that we were getting bored, so he asked us the same question! He didn't tell us the answer—the question was good enough. It kind of made me think. MAHOGANY

> Our teacher asked, "What does the word 'civilized' mean to you?" I thought about that the whole marking period. For our journal writing, he asked us, "Are humans born naturally mean? Are humans naturally savages?" I don't think they're born that way, but they develop it. MONTOYA

Challenge our assumptions.

> My teacher asked us: What does "ghetto" mean to you? I thought it was like kids from Oakland, but she told us it was about Jews. Also I used to think black people were all drug dealers, but my history teacher said: "Have you ever thought about how much people [went through] to get here?" It made me change the way I thought about them. VERONICA

I thought black people were the only people that were in slavery, but we learned that lots of people had been enslaved. PORSCHE

We were learning the Holocaust and some people made funny side comments about it. The teacher asked, "What gives you the right to say that?" Then people started thinking about it, and apologizing. I guess that made them think differently about it. LUIS

Don't stick to textbooks.

It helps to supplement boring reading with other materials that may be about the same subject but are more interesting or easy to get into. In my U.S. history class we had the standard boring textbook, but the teacher also gave us some lighter, more interesting articles that helped me not get bogged down. Videos are also good. HILARY

Textbooks might be trying to indoctrinate you into what society wants you to know. Our history teacher had like fifty textbooks in the room, and we were supposed to look through and compare what they said about the same event, like the American Revolution. Even if the dates were the same, the interpretations were all different and some were even incorrect. We use evidence and actual documents instead. ALEXIS

Sometimes the teachers feel their hands are tied and bound to the book. Like in my old school we had to study for the [state exams]. My history teacher had been in Japan, and he had been in the army and traveled all over the world. He could have tied his experiences to the Ming dynasty but instead he had to close off talking about what he knew and get back to the subject. That's when a person's love for teaching comes out, when they get to talk about something they know. VANCE

Help us with resources. When we have research projects, make sure everyone has access to research sources like the library and the Internet, and time at school to use them.

> Research can be done in class—spread it out. You can go to the library every day for a week. ANDRES

Give us time to think, to draft, and to revise.

> If you're going to put it on the test and it's going to be a difficult question, give us a chance to think about it first in class. MARIBEL

> For essays it works good when we have a certain time to do the first draft—not overnight! Then, after the teacher looks at it, we do it again. For me the issue is give me time. Then I wouldn't have such a problem turning it in on time. DIANA

> I never learned how to write a paper except by introduction, body, conclusion. When I got to high school, I didn't know how to compare three books. So my teachers always told me new ways to do it. They would say: Here, you can have a tape recorder. Or: Don't give me a paper, just write what you think about these three books and then we can think about how to organize it. So I'm not afraid anymore. I'm smart—I say some good things but I'm the type that if I do it and it's not right, I don't want to hand it in. They told me, Yo! Hand it in and we'll sit down with you and we can work on it. ALEXIS

ENCOURAGING ACTIVE LEARNING

It's always easier to learn complicated concepts by doing things, not just by having someone talk about the ideas.

> I like activities. We're all different learners—some people are visual learners, some hands-on, and some more able to do book work. So it helps all kinds of people understand. MAHOGANY

> In one class they asked us what we would do if we crashed on an island in an airplane, and only the students were left. One girl said she would be the leader. Who's going to be the farmer, who will kill the animals? One of the students got sick with malaria and we had to find a weed plant that would cure her. VERONICA

As we noted in Chapter 5, working in groups often helps students learn through their own actions and inquiry, rather than by passively listening.

> Our math teacher gives us an assignment to work on in groups. We have 40 minutes, and we write on big poster paper how we solved it and the answer. Then at the end we give five-minute presentations to the rest of the class, and he evaluates them. Sometimes people solve it a different way, or get the answer wrong, and you can learn from that. ANDRES

But for this kind of active learning to really work, teachers need to keep in mind several things:

Use students as interpreters of other students' problems.

> Sometimes a kid is trying to ask a question and the teacher seems not to understand at all, but another kid will understand and be able to help. HILARY

> In my math class my teacher puts about four or five people at a table. At each table there is at least one person who does really good in math, kind of like a captain, who helps you if you get stuck. MAHOGANY

Choose group work with care. Make sure it can actually evoke the concepts teachers want students to explore.

> My junior-year math class had two seniors as student teaching assistants, and we worked on a few problems in groups with their help only. For it to work, [the teacher] had to pick really well-thought-out problems that would help you learn it. He had to put a lot of thought into how he chose the questions. HILARY

Monitor and assess groups as they work together. Stay aware of whether all students are pulling their weight and learning the material. (See Chapter 5 for suggestions on how to do this.)

> One of my science teachers constantly put me in groups with people who didn't want to work. Later she told me she thought I could push them to work. What's the point if I have to do it myself anyway? MAHOGANY

> It happens a lot that you end up in a group where only two out of four do the work. HILARY

Don't leave students to learn entirely on their own. At some point the teacher needs to get more involved and check that students really understand.

> We have a lot of assignments where we look up the information and then explain it to the class. It's a good way to get comfortable with talking in front of the class, but I don't think it's always the best way to learn. The

students might leave things out, or sometimes they don't really know the subject and the teacher has to correct them. And some things can't be explained by students as well as they can be by teachers. DIANA

At some point you can't learn that much from other kids talking all the time. A lot of kids didn't take it seriously, or they didn't have a lot of time to prepare, or they didn't emphasize the right points. So it's not fair. You need the teacher to provide continuity, tie it all together, explain it better. HILARY

KNOWING WHEN STUDENTS UNDERSTAND

Students feel a lot of anxiety about mastering difficult material, especially when a lot depends on their doing so. They know that understanding a subject well will help them when they go on to further studies, for one thing. They sense that they learn more when teachers prod them into active inquiry rather than merely telling them what they have to know. But also they realize that a standardized exit exam, a College Board exam, or a high school grade point average can have a big impact on their immediate future.

If you're raised by teachers just telling you things and forcing them on you, it's hard or frustrating when teachers expect you to be proactive and take responsibility for your own education. VANCE

That underlines the need for a teacher to find out whether a student really understands difficult material *and* to prepare them to perform well on high-stakes tests. These goals may not overlap, students realize, and so they suggest a mix of actions:

Ask for feedback. Make sure we have a chance to let you know how we're doing, whether it's through informal discussions, journal writing, or a suggestion box. We often worry that our grades will suffer if we admit to not understanding something, so provide some kind of reassurance or anonymity.

> Ask while there's still time, don't wait till the end. The student knows after the first month how the class goes and what's the routine, but it's still early enough to change it. What's hazy for you, what's hard for you, what has stuck with you that you really understood? VANCE

> Ask us if we feel we've improved and what we've learned. Sometimes teachers can be really duped. They think they're really reaching kids, but they're really boring. [They] wouldn't necessarily know that from the expression on our face. MIKA

Use class assessments that let us show we understand the things that matter. Quizzes, tests, and project presentations should be designed to demonstrate that we have mastered important concepts, not trivial things. Make it clear early on what the criteria are, so we can prepare to show what we know.

> Just test the things that are interesting and important, or the ones that relate to exams that outside people are going to be testing. ALEXIS

Put standardized tests into perspective. When a test can make or break us, it's only fair to prepare us for it. But we should know the difference, because the things that help us really learn often take a lot of time. Be honest about when and why you are giving test prep priority.

> [When tests are coming up soon, teachers] can't always ask the students to try to figure out what they're trying to get across. It's more like: Here's

the material, if you have any questions you're free to come ask. The other way—when they give us clues and have us try to figure it out—is too time consuming. BOSUNG

MAKING SENSE OF DIFFICULT MATH AND SCIENCE

For lots of reasons, helping teenagers learn math and science is one of the hardest things for teachers—and students!—to agree on. For one thing, teachers of math and science argue among themselves on the best ways to teach. Major differences also show up among the different textbooks and tests, so it's hard to know which approach to choose. It gets even more complicated because kids "get" these subjects via very different learning paths, yet many teachers prefer to stick to the way they themselves learn best. Finally, advances in these subjects are coming so fast that teachers often are not experts in the field. The current teacher shortage in math and science makes that even worse.

Like teachers, our student co-authors do not always agree on how best to help kids learn in these two areas. Their advice sometimes reflects that tension but nonetheless falls into several principles that most believe hold true.

Walk us through things. When presenting a new idea, give us an introduction first. Don't leave us entirely on our own.

> Sometimes teachers just leave you to do it. They give you a problem set and don't really explain it. If you're teaching a formula or a new method to solve math, leave problems on the board. Or have handouts that take it step by step and use the same formula on several different problems. ANDRES

> He doesn't want to tell us how to do it—he wants us to figure out for ourselves. It's hard, it's frustrating. It feels like he's not teaching. But

then after we've got our minds and our juices flowing, he'll tell us. And then he'll put another couple of problems on the board and move on. He doesn't treat us like children. That's where the frustration is, because students are used to that. We're like, "Break it down for me!" And he says, "Break it down yourself." ALEXIS

Try all different ways to see something. We need to have a lot of ways to approach a problem.

We have a computer program and it works well with math. They give you the word problem, and you have to graph it. It helps because you can see the graph. MAHOGANY

Use a lot of concrete examples. Don't start with formulas. Instead, look for everyday illustrations of math or science concepts, like the angle of our shadows or the arc of a basketball.

It doesn't work when we just sit and take notes on different terms. It has to be more real than that. Science and math are so conceptual that at times it's hard to comprehend, so students need concrete analogies or examples. LATIA

For physics we had to analyze a movie. I watched *The Matrix* and talked about why he wouldn't be able to jump from one building to another because of friction. I enjoyed it because you got to apply your knowledge and see how physics mattered in the world. It was fun and I was applying my knowledge. DARYL

In A.P. Statistics they had to do a survey on how many people in the school had cellular phones. They got to pick the topic. MAHOGANY

Give us plenty of practice, but not just drills.

> Don't think students just get it after the first time. Keep repeating a new thing and blend it in with the other stuff that you do. LUIS

> If you learn a new formula, send us home with two or three problems that use it. Once we've figured out what to do, we get bored with drills. ANDRES

Don't rely too much on the textbook.

> When things in the textbook seem really boring, do activities that force us to get involved and make connections. In my ninth-grade science class we read about how resources were divided among the world, and he had students act as countries and divide up popcorn in amounts that represented their country's share of the resources. We had to organize to get enough popcorn for our countries. DARYL

Help us along when we're discouraged. When we just can't seem to figure out a problem or grasp a concept, we need your supportive coaching.

> I got lost in my math class—this one little thing, "SOHCAHTOA," got me off track.[*] He sees that a couple of students understand it and he assumes we all do, and he moves on. I don't feel comfortable asking for help. He's so intent on moving ahead that he doesn't make a space for us to ask. LAURALIZ

> I was making the question too hard—I was thinking too much! LATIA

---

[*]A mnemonic device used in trigonometry classes to remind students via an anagram that "For a right triangle, the Sine of an angle equals the ratio of the length of the side Opposite that angle to the length of the Hypotenuse; the Cosine equals the ratio of the length of the side Adjacent to that angle to the length of the Hypotenuse; the Tangent equals the ratio of the length of the side Opposite that angle to the length of the side Adjacent to that angle."

BRINGING DIFFICULT LITERATURE ALIVE

Literature also brings its share of controversy to teachers. Considering the enormous cultural diversity of American public-school teenagers, for example, should they be reading mostly works that reflect the Eurocentric canon? How can a teacher help all students, even those whose English-language skills are just developing, gain full access to the world of print? What role does literacy in the arts play in opening a range of expression to students? How can literature help teenagers explore the meaning of their own lives?

We have already addressed some of these issues in Chapter 6, in the section where students talk about what motivates them to read and write. Other issues come up in Chapter 8, as students who are still learning English as their second language speak of their challenges in this area. Just as with math and science, students do not always agree on what best helps them take on difficult material in reading and get something out of it. But from their experiences, they offer these insights and advice:

Make clear why you chose a piece for us to read.

> It's for a reason. Point out the interesting things in it. Like when she says about *Henry IV* that it's a coming-of-age story about a prince who breaks away from his royalty, that helps. At least you don't feel like they're just giving it to you to waste your time and get on your nerves. TIFFANY

Break down complex reading into parts.

> When you're reading something you're not interested in, it takes you forever to read it, maybe 20 minutes to read five pages. In my class we're reading *Henry IV*, the stupidest thing that Shakespeare ever wrote.

Our teacher knows we don't like it, so she assigns about half the usual amount. Then every day when we come in to class, she guides us to make sure we're keeping up with the story line. TIFFANY

Relate the reading to our lives.

Bring in current movies, texts, or debates that relate to what the reading is. Like relate *Romeo and Juliet* to interracial dating, or with *Jane Eyre*, talk about how single women are viewed in our society. DARYL

For me I have to translate it into things to get involved with the book. I hated Gatsby, but [it would have been better] if they had [presented him as] some kid who grew up and didn't have a lot, and he liked a girl who always had the best of things and always dated men who had the best of things, and then one day he made it. LATIA

In the beginning I didn't like *The Great Gatsby* at all. But the teacher compared it to our lives, she brought it into our time. It's about old money and new money—Tom had old money passed down and cheated on his wife. She warmed us up to it, and in the end I liked it. MAHOGANY

Link literature to the lives of other people we can meet.

We had to read *A Separate Peace*, and part of it is about World War II, so the teacher had us find someone in our neighborhood who had lived through that war. I found this neat old woman half a block away—her first husband, who she had only been married to a couple of months, had died in the war. It was neat that she talked about that, and I guess I remember the book better because of it. HILARY

Find out why we don't like a particular literary work.

> Different students don't like different books for different reasons. If we're reading *Jane Eyre*, I might not like it because it's stupid, and Daryl might not like it because it's too long. There was no helping that book. TIFFANY

Take our interpretations seriously.

> We read a lot of Thomas Hobbes and talked about it in class. We had to connect it to *Lord of the Flies*. I felt like what he said was important, about whether people need authority, and I had something to say about it. I think I disagreed with him. It was interesting. I felt really good about writing about a philosopher. MONTOYA

Introduce us to different people's interpretations.

> Sometimes when the teacher is talking about symbolism and that kind of thing, you think they don't know what they're talking about. There's more than one interpretation, so try to get somebody else's opinion about what it means. Having the person visit who actually wrote it would be interesting, or reading the author's commentary. DARYL

Use drama and props to help us visualize the world of the book.

> Artifacts or music can be good. My teacher brought in a spear when we were reading *Things Fall Apart*, and asked us how we would feel if people who we didn't agree with just invaded our home. VANCE

TIPS ON HELPING US READ DIFFICULT ACADEMIC MATERIAL

- The teacher and the students should read the book out loud in class. If they don't understand, stop, talk, and look it up. LUIS

- I don't like when the teacher reads out loud to the class, especially in an annoying voice. I feel like a little kid. And I hate having kids read out loud if they can't read well. TIFFANY

- If the vocabulary is difficult, make games about it. There's a game with passing a ball around with a definition, it helps you learn the words together. Or work in partners and talk about it. VERONICA

- Get students to ask questions about the book, to write something about the book—a summary, or their observations and questions. LUIS

- Make up a fun game or project that has to do with the book. MONTOYA

- Drawing something about the book helps you understand what's going on—it gets you more involved with the book. It really helps to take a strong quote from the book and then make a drawing of it. LUIS

- Connect the reading to the students' life somehow. Maybe have a class or group reading where everyone reads together. ANDRES

- Make a play to go with the book. DIANA

- After reading the book, watch the movie and talk about which you liked more. We did that with *Lord of the Flies*. I think the book was better. LUIS

- Break it up into parts. Assign small amounts of reading a night, and have a small quiz on them the next day. DIANA

We did *Romeo and Juliet* as a play; we broke it up into parts and memo-rized the scenes. I played Juliet and I had the balcony scene: "Romeo, Romeo, wherefore art thou Romeo . . . [quotes ten lines of verse]." DIANA

Design activities to do with the book.

You can give an assignment to change the book somehow. Maybe change the ending, or write a spin-off story about a character. Do role playing, like in *Jane Eyre*, take the part of Mr. Rochester. What was he doing when Jane Eyre went away? TIFFANY

To help us get the feeling in *Romeo and Juliet*, our teacher told us to write our own plays about conflicts in families. LAURALIZ

Use movies, but not as substitutes for reading.

The movie will cut things out and change a novel, but you could have discussions about what different versions and interpretations mean and what you think of them. VANCE

I really wanted to read *Othello* because I had seen a little bit of the movie *O*, and I had been told that it's a really good play. Our teacher had us read Act 1 for a month, then we watched the play as a movie for three acts, then she moved on. We didn't get to finish the book, and we should have. LAURALIZ

CARING ABOUT HISTORY

History and social studies, like literature, sometimes seem to teenagers like a mountain of material to master, with little incentive to do so except graduation requirements and standardized tests. But here, too, student co-authors offer their experiences as guidance:

Help us visualize history. Finding real people to come and talk about their experiences makes history come alive. In times too long past for that, role-plays can make people and situations in history more immediate.

> One time this actor came in as a person from the Civil War—the teacher didn't even announce it. He came in his Confederate uniform, and he stayed in character; he denied that he was an actor. We started out trying to prove that he wasn't what he was, but by doing that we ended up learning a lot about the Civil War. VANCE

Focus on the most important questions, not just on names and dates.

> When you hear the story of the Pilgrims, it seems like they came, they were hungry, the Indians helped them. There was Thanksgiving, it was all nice. When my old teachers would tell it, I wouldn't understand why the Pilgrims would hate the Indians if they gave them food. But my teacher explained how the Pilgrims resented the Native Americans for helping them. It was a matter of white pride, Christian pride, jealousy, envy—human emotions and motives. That connected it to me. I could identify. History still affects us; people who were once in conflict had children. VANCE

Don't rely on lectures or textbooks. Instead, collect interesting documents and articles that will get us interested in finding out more through research.

> Reading history textbooks was incredibly boring. But in U.S. History we learned that *The Wizard of Oz* is an allegory for the populist movement in America in the 1920s, when the U.S. was moving toward big government. Dorothy represented the common man and the Wizard was representing failed promises. She gave us an an article and we talked about that. HILARY

HOW TO USE MOVIES AND VIDEOS

Do...	Don't...
Use a film as background to bring a subject alive. Documentaries or dramas showing historical events or eras, different versions of Shakespeare plays, or videos on issues in science can help clarify those subjects and make them more interesting.	**Use a film as a stand-in for teaching.** Anything you show should contribute to what the class is supposed to learn.
Suggest important questions to focus on during the film. If it's a film on the guillotine, ask, "Is capital punishment right in a democratic society?"	**Show films too often.** They shouldn't turn into a substitute for more active classes. We can tell when teachers use films because they're not prepared.
Follow a film with discussion and writing. What questions and responses did it provoke in us? If based on a book, how did it differ? Sometimes a mini-quiz will help us keep focused on the movie instead of tuning out.	**Show films in place of reading literary texts.** Movies often distort the character of the book they're based on. Get us to compare the film and the print versions, and to think about the reasons for their differences.

Seek out our opinions and make us defend them. Have debates where we take sides and argue about issues in history and social studies. Using evidence to support our side is a good incentive to do research and think critically about historical interpretations.

> We had to write about blood diamonds in Africa. My paper was on the Cuban embargo. After researching it, I had an opinion to express about it, and I had to figure out how to express it in the most persuasive way. DARYL

TEACHERS AS LEARNERS, TOO

A teacher's attitude toward scholarship plays a huge role in helping students learn to value difficult academic work. Students recognize when a teacher has passion for his or her field, is eager to learn new things, and brings genuine questions into the classroom for them to explore as partners. Even when teachers are not experts in a particular field, the way they react will send a powerful message to kids about the value of curiosity, hard work, and lifelong learning.

> It helps if teachers let the students know there are gaps in their knowledge—students can often fill in those gaps and learn from doing it. It's great if teachers say that they are learning with the students, especially with something like history or English where students have prior knowledge and can share that. But there are limitations to that, and teachers always should know where to go to do more research and learning on their own. This is another thing they should share with students—where to go to find more information about the material. Be curious and share that with students—talk together about things you don't know and want to learn about the subject. HILARY

Summary

TEACHING DIFFICULT MATERIAL

- Find out what we know already and link it to new material.

- Break down complicated material.

- Try different ways to approach things.

- Ask questions that really make us think.

- Challenge our assumptions.

- Don't stick to textbooks.

- Help us with resources.

- Give us time to think, to draft, and to revise.

CHAPTER 8

Teaching Teenagers Who Are Still Learning English

"SOMETIMES I DON'T KNOW HOW TO EXPRESS WHO I AM."

How can teachers work effectively with a class full of high school students whose English is limited? This question had particular relevance to us as we developed this chapter, most of whose student co-authors were still separated into an "English-language development" class in a large Bay Area high school.

These twenty students came from twelve different countries. Some had arrived the very week we visited their class to ask their advice. Others had studied for two or three years in this same classroom, always aiming to pass the tests that would move them into "regular" academic classes. Ranging in age from fourteen to seventeen, they came from extremely different academic backgrounds. Donnel would have been graduating from high school in the Philippines, and going on to college. Sam had lived in the Bay Area all his life, but spoke only Korean at home. The students from Brazil had a rigorous school experience behind them; the students from China had grown up with strict cultural rules for teacher-student interactions. Several students came from Mexico and Peru, with varying amounts of previous schooling.

As they gathered eagerly to offer their thoughts and advice to new teachers, they stumbled and hesitated over their words. Sam cast his eyes down in painful shyness, filling page after page of a notebook with pencil sketches of the world in his head—people, castles, dogs. Cynthia, fresh from Guatemala, stuck closely to a girlfriend, the two murmuring continually in Spanish. Pedro, recently arrived from Mexico, relied on Javier and Rafael to elaborate on his two- or three-word replies. Elaine spilled out her answers urgently, passionately speaking her mind despite the grammatical errors she knew she was making.

This Bay Area class reflects national trends. At least one in every six adolescents going to school in the United States comes from a family in which English is not the main language—and that percentage is increasing, according to U.S. Census Bureau projections. These 3.4 million teenagers have faces as varied as twenty-first-century America. In many urban schools these days, one can easily count more than one hundred first languages among the student body.

Behind these statistics is a mosaic of individual teenagers like these, each struggling to grow up and find a place in the world. That challenge can feel lonely and painful in the most comfortable of social settings, but for newcomers to this country whose English is just developing, it is even harder.

> It's difficult for us because we don't make a lot of friends. You just make ELD [English-language development] friends, because we be afraid about talking wrong English with other students who speak English. That makes it harder to learn to speak English, if we have no chance to speak. ELAINE

> Sometimes they laugh if you want to [try to speak English with them]. But sometimes you're upset and you don't feel like laughing. MURILO

> Sometimes I don't know how to express who I am to people. BARBARA

How can a teacher best help these teenagers learn? Students addressed this question with the utmost seriousness—making lists of advice, telling their own stories, comparing and analyzing their experiences as learners in a new language. Their commitment to that work itself vividly answered the question.

DRAWING OUT WHAT STUDENTS KNOW

Finding out as much as possible about students' lives, both past and present, helps a teacher make important connections between things kids already know and what they will be learning in class. It's easier to remember new words and ways if they build on or compare to experiences students already have. Analogies, pictures, photographs, movies, and television can help make these connections and provide background information in a variety of subject areas. Below, students list some things they wished teachers knew about them.

WHO ARE WE?
What Students Learning English Wish Teachers Would Ask

Where are you from?

When did you come to this country?

What languages do you speak already?

What was your last school like? What kinds of things did you study?

Did you learn English in your country before you came?

Does your family speak English at home?

Do you have someone to help you with schoolwork at home?

What do you do after school?

Do you play sports?

Do you work at a job?

What other classes do you take?

What kind of food do you like to eat?

Do you have any health problems the teacher should know about?

How do you feel about living in this country?

Do you want to learn English? If so, why? If not, why not?

Do you read in English? If so, what do you read?

Do you like to read in your own language? If so, what do you read?

Do you watch TV? If so, what?

Do you feel comfortable in this school? If so, why? If not, why not?

What else do you like to do?

Teachers probably won't be able to collect this information all at once simply by handing out a written questionnaire. Instead, they might find things out in more informal ways (like conversations before and after class, or in journal assignments). But even while presenting academic content, teachers can draw students into conversation about their attitudes and experiences. For example, student co-authors said they might contribute ideas in class discussions like these:

In a class that studies . . .	English-language learners might talk about . . .
Reading and writing	What stories and legends "everyone knows" in the cultures they come from, and how those are passed along.
Civics	How leaders come to power in their country of origin. If through elections, what is the voting age?
History	The immigration experience of various ethnic groups in America, and their struggles for recognition and rights.
Science	What technologies people use in everyday life in their home cultures (for building, communication, transportation, medicine, agriculture, and so on) and how they came into use.
Math	What currencies people use in their native countries and how to convert that currency into dollars. Charts, graphs, and other ways of showing statistics about ethnicities represented in the school, the state, the nation.
Geography	The geographical location and features of their homelands.
Home economics	The food and feast traditions in their cultures.
Spanish	The connections between Spanish vocabulary, grammar, and literary genres and those in English and other languages. Comparing figurative language, wordplay, pronunciation, or other linguistic subtleties in languages other than English.

Making such links gives a clear message that teachers value the cultures students come from—and that they, too, expect to learn from the class. Students can then start to feel like legitimate experts in some areas and respected apprentices in others. (See below for specific suggestions.)

Once teachers know more about their students' skills, they can create situations in which students interact more naturally with classmates whose first language is English.

> My first English teacher in middle school saw me and my friend dancing and she made a class after school for us to teach samba to English-speaking kids. Teachers can make connections for us if they know what we can do. ELAINE

> I think some teachers [should] send [students to be our] buddies. They should tell them we need to make friends and we want to but we don't know how. We could learn from them. I want to learn their culture and their language. And they could learn my culture and my language. ELAINE

BUILDING BRIDGES BETWEEN CULTURES

When asked, our student collaborators who were just learning English eagerly shared details of their lives in their home cultures. But such conversation rarely occurred in the context of their regular classes, they said. They tried to imagine ways in which a teacher might invite such conversation, encouraging them to learn while at the same time building bridges from their first culture to their new one. For example, they suggested:

- Connect your own family's immigration experience to what we face today. When did your family arrive in this country? What challenges did they meet?

- Explore with us the values of our families and communities—not just ours, but yours. What do we consider most important, and how can you tell?

- Help us analyze why some immigrants succeed while others fail. Bring issues like racism into the classroom as subjects.

- Teach us the ways things work in America (who can vote, or what rights we have). But also ask how our native countries approach things like school schedules, homework, or teenagers working.

- Help us negotiate the problems we face in and out of school. Ask us to research our own neighborhoods through topics like drug abuse, intergenerational conflicts, homelessness, teenage pregnancy, or environmental hazards.

- Ask us what we think about the books we read and the curriculum we must study.

- Learn how we say things in our language.

- Let us be translators for others in our culture—both adults and other students—so their voices can also be heard.

- Respect us!

LOOKING PAST LANGUAGE MISTAKES

Understandably, English-language learners may be particularly sensitive to whether or not adults show respect for their abilities.

> When I first came to this country in middle school, I had science and the teacher gave tests for everybody. He said, "You can write?" Then he gave you the answers—this and this and this. I felt bad because I didn't do the test, he did my test. MURILO

> I take a class for Hispanic students, to make their Spanish better for school. The teacher treats us like we're a lot younger than we are. Like:

"We're going to play a game—spin the dial and point it to a continent! And she's all excited, and we're like, "How many minutes are left in the class?" She talks really slow, like: "You spell this word A–G–U–A." I already know Spanish! It's my first language! VERONICA

My first year in science class, the teacher gave me a test and he said, "I think you can't do this test because you don't speak English, but anyway I will give you a B if you come every day." I started to cry—he assume that I couldn't do it, and I felt really bad. Because I feel comfortable when I study and take a good grade and say, "I did this." ELAINE

It's crucial to recognize that for English-language learners, succeeding in an American classroom goes well beyond just comprehending what a teacher says. Our co-authors suggested several general guidelines for teaching students with limited English, most of which, in one way or another, touch on the issue of respect.

Focus on the important thinking we do, not just language mistakes. Help us learn the words we need to express "why?" or "how?" or "how do we know?"

In our regular classes [the students with limited English] know a lot [even though] they have this big accent. They try really hard, they work even harder. It's inspiring! LAURALIZ

Share our goal to excel academically, not just get by.

I [prefer] higher classes to learn more. PEDRO

You can take more advanced classes, but for sure you will not get good grades, but more classes use more advanced words—but it makes you feel better, you're not so bored. RAFAEL

The teacher can help me get into the right classes, and get into college as soon as I can. DONNEL

Make connections between academic content and our own experience. Help us do real things that matter to us.

When I was in history class I learned something about justice—about the Bill of Rights. They took a while. When my teacher talked about human rights, we talked about what rights we had. JAVIER

I want to become an auto mechanic some day. The teacher can help me learn to use computers and to find opportunities. And teach me English words so I know how to explain car trouble to people. JAVIER

Help us enter real and important texts—but at a level we can handle. Model an activity or assignment with a small group of students while we watch to see how it is done. Give us opportunities to make drafts and revise our work after feedback.

I was put in ESL and I was pulled out to read, and we would read really easy books. We could read already, and it was insulting. You were like the outcasts, and that made me mad. DIANA

If I can't understand, I ask them. I say please show me [with gestures]. TSUGUMI

Help us understand the secrets of "book language." Teach us what to look for when we read—words that indicate comparisons, or chapter subheads, or illustrations and charts. Before we read, give us a preview of what important vocabulary to watch for.

You can learn more words and that will help [you] learn more complicated ideas. MURILO

Colleges use more complicated words and so it's better to learn them now. [It's] difficult but good to listen, because your ear gets used to it. XIMENA

Teach us to take risks in our new language. Help us analyze when it's easy to talk English and when it's hard.

When I came to this English class I started to write papers with the word "because"—now I did it so much that I am bored with "because." We have to change and learn more—if you learn, you have to go to the next step. ELAINE

Last semester I took a math analysis class, and most of the time I didn't really understand. I just sit right there and are quiet and took notes. KAREN

Give us alternative methods to present our knowledge. Use not just language but math, computers, video, music, art, and movement as legitimate means of expression.

In one project in my math class we made air rockets. Working in pairs, it's fairly simple to make, and you don't need a lot of talking to understand what you're going to do next. ANDRES

Help us learn from each other. Don't worry about a noisy classroom—we need to talk!

> Sometimes we know what they don't know and we can explain to others.
> JAVIER

> They send some people as volunteer aides to sit with students who don't speak the language and help them through the work. There's a girl in my English class who doesn't speak any English at all, so they sit me next to her and get me to talk to her because I speak Spanish. VERONICA

Don't be afraid to let us use our own language as we figure things out.

> If you just switch straight to English, you have a lot of trouble. I used to only speak Spanish at home, until fifth or sixth grade, and then I went to an elementary school and middle school where half my classes were taught in Spanish and half in English. That helped my English get better. In middle school I was still doing better in Spanish, but by the time I went to high school my English was fine except for spelling, because that's kind of hard to learn in English. Now I want to be a writer—in English, not Spanish—and I read more things in English than in Spanish.
> ANDRES

CLASSROOM BEHAVIOR AND LANGUAGE FATIGUE

Teachers should stay extra aware of the emotional fatigue that language-minority adolescents experience every day. First, they must bear the strain of sitting through classes in which they do not understand everything they hear. Not every term or acronym in a school's common parlance can even be found in a dictionary.

> In the middle school I got three suspensions—a lot of it because I didn't understand. The first one: I don't speak English and I go to lunch and I cut the line. Everyone said, "You can't cut the line, and for punishment I give you a 'wooz.'" I didn't know what it was and I didn't go—you have to clean the school, pick up garbage. And then he gave me a slip and the next day I went to the office. They gave me a "sac"—it's a class, you have to read a book, and write something more than five hundred words, watch a movie. I didn't know what it was, and I didn't go. And then they suspended me. MURILO

In addition, newcomers must often learn the everyday techniques of American high schools—using textbooks, taking useful notes, doing research. These habits may differ considerably from the way they "did school" in their previous situation.

As a result, when students zone out or act up in class, don't assume that students are showing apathy or disrespect; seek other explanations for the behavior. Our co-authors came up with a list of ways in which they act out the stress of not understanding what's going on in class. (See list on page 156.)

Boys and girls may act differently in response to such strain. Because of deep-rooted stereotypes about masculinity, a boy may be even more sensitive to possible loss of face, or take action to relieve his stress.

> It's more difficult for a boy. Girls get along better with people, but boys always say who is the best. I am a Mexican so they have discrimination already [here] from white or black. JAVIER

HOW WE ACT WHEN WE DON'T UNDERSTAND WHAT'S SAID IN CLASS

We cry when we're scared.

We make a face—roll our eyes.

We put our heads down and sleep.

We get angry—we kick the chair, we say bad words.

We interrupt and talk loud.

We cut class.

We daydream in class, don't pay attention, think of other things.

We ask the counselor if we can drop the class, because we're afraid.

We bite our nails.

We listen to music.

We feel hungry.

We fight with other students.

We bother the other students.

We flirt with the other students.

We stay home.

We run away.

What can teachers do when they suspect that students are reacting to language fatigue with behavior like this? Students suggested these responses:

Always ask us if we understand.

> Repeat [things], because most of the time we don't understand everything. Explain again if they don't. Or ask the student to stay after school and explain. ELAINE

> Talk to them after class. Ask if everything is okay. If they have some problem, get a translator! If you can't find a translator, get a student translator. ELAINE

Listen carefully to discover what we need help with.

I don't find the correct words to express yourself, and so some people who only speak English, they don't understand. XIMENA

Try to make the class fun, using different teaching approaches.

Most of the times you get bored when it's too much information for your mind. You have to mix fun stuff and hard stuff to keep the interest level. RAFAEL

See through angry behavior to its causes.

It's hard—you get someone when they're really angry. MARCOS

You just can help him if he wants help. If he doesn't, it won't help. If we show him, maybe he changes a lot. In my first year I didn't care a lot, I acted out. Then people came and talk about college in class and other students, and adults, talked to me. ELAINE

Have patience.

If you don't have a patient teacher, it's bad. If the teacher can't make you understand, he gives up on you and stops trying. RAFAEL

Sometimes teachers get angry if the student doesn't understand after two times. They speak in loud voices, [or] they give a zero sometimes. ELAINE

Teachers who take the time and trouble to do these things will gain the trust of their students in return. For their part, students learn to believe in themselves,

HELP US SUCCEED! What We Need and Why We Need It

	Long-term dream	How teacher can help with it	Short-term hope	How teacher can help with it
Rafael	To be successful at everything—money, love; maybe become an architect	Show me the different kinds of professions, help me find out the colleges with the things I am interested in.	To be accepted next year at college in San Diego	Be my counselor
Pedro	To be a plumber	Help make the connection with the people who have work	To take a class at a school for plumbers, study more, learn the skills of business; to learn better English	Bring in a list of plumbing terms so I know them
Tsugumi	To be an English teacher in Japan	Help me find a school to prepare me to get a teacher's license	Next year I have to go back to Japan	Help me learn good English and pronunciation
Javier	To become an auto mechanic	Use computers to connect to car work, use connections to help find opportunities	To learn how to use a computer better	Teach me more English so I know how to explain car trouble to people
Jae Yoon	To be a mechanical engineer	Be a good friend, stay in touch, support over the long term. Maybe by that time I can do something for her too.	To speak more English, learn writing, reading, speaking	I already learned a lot of math in Korea but I could learn more here. Teach me more English that has to do with my interests
Krishneel	To become a professional soccer player, maybe a businessman	Both people have to be thinking [about it], not just me but the teacher	Play soccer next year; speak more English	Helping me with English
Elaine	To finish university; maybe become a translator or teach languages	Help me find the right university; explain what classes I need to take to get there	Finish all four years of high school English by senior year	Give me good information, things to read, new words; tell me what summer or night classes will help; be my friend!
Sam	To have a job related to art or crafts	Help me learn about careers in art; help set up an internship	Take art class for the first time; improve my English	Locate art class; learn other skills like computer
Brian	To be an Air Force jet pilot	Connect me with opportunities	Get grades in courses helpful for entry to Air Force	Connect me with the right courses
Kirandeep	To become a doctor	Connect me with people in the medical field to learn more	Get good grades in the hardest classes I can take	Help me get into the right classes
Donnel	To be an architect or a composer	Help me get to college as soon as possible	Get into college as soon as I can	Help me get into the right classes

to take risks, and to seek out help when they confront obstacles, both in the classroom and outside it.

> In P.E. class one boy put his hands on my body and I started to cry. I went everywhere trying to find someone, a teacher, who could understand what I was saying. [Finally I] explained everything to my Spanish teacher, and I asked her to talk to my counselor. She translated, and they showed me pictures [until I could identify the boy] and then they called him in and talked to the boy. I talked it out with him—I said, "Don't do it again." He said, "The other girls don't mind," and I said: "Just know you have all different people here." ELAINE

THE SPECIAL CHALLENGE OF WRITING WELL

For non-English speakers, writing well in English poses a tremendous challenge. And though students with limited English should work toward the same standards as the rest of the class, it's fair for a teacher to adapt the writing task or vary the requirements for demonstrating success to acknowledge their greater effort. For example, English-language learners could produce one piece (or sentence, or paragraph) that meets the writing standards, while others in the class produce several. Or they could demonstrate content mastery in an oral presentation or another medium.

Even in a diverse group, students without strong writing skills can contribute a great deal to the thinking involved in a writing project, while soaking up both process and product by observing better writers. This symbiotic relationship builds positive mutual regard on both sides.

Some teachers use the following approach, known as 1-2-4-Share, which incorporates brainstorming, critique, revision, and reflection into a group process.

1-2-4-SHARE: A GROUP WRITING PROCESS

■ First, each student makes notes on what he or she might want to say.

■ Then each student gets together with a partner to share ideas and feedback and to combine ideas they both agree on into a joint written version. (Less strong writers thus have the benefit of a partner who can help express their ideas more clearly.)

■ Each pair then joins with another pair, forming a group of four that repeats the process of sharing, critique, and co-writing, to create a new written piece. In this group, an observer takes notes on the group's process of reaching agreement and writing the paper.

■ Each group of four then presents the final piece to the class.

■ The observers report to the class on each group's process.

TEACHING FOR THE FUTURE

Even more than for other students, teachers can unlock the future for students who are still learning a new language and culture. If they take the time to find out their students' hopes and dreams, they can help in all kinds of practical and academic ways, both short term and long term. Students are hungry for this kind of help, as they show in the chart on page 158. Teachers' actions and respect can give these students the motivation and encouragement to keep trying in the face of enormous frustration.

In trying to act on the suggestions of the students in this chapter, the following questions make a good daily reflection for teachers:

Did my students understand the work we did today? How do I know?

What did I do today to acknowledge their strengths and achievements?

What did I learn today about my students and their cultures?

How could I use what I learned to connect to their learning?

Summary

TEACHING ENGLISH-LANGUAGE LEARNERS

- Focus on the important thinking we do, not just language mistakes.

- Share our goal to excel academically, not just get by.

- Make connections between academic content and our own experiences.

- Give us real and important texts to read—but at a level we can handle.

- Help us understand the secrets of "book language."

- Teach us to take risks in our new language.

- Give us alternative methods to present our knowledge.

- Help us learn from each other.

- Don't be afraid to let us use our own language as we figure things out.

CHAPTER 9

When Things Go Wrong

"Try your best, don't give up."

The dark days of school, for both students and teachers, come with discouraging frequency. Learning involves failure. In large groups teenagers typically create smaller alliances to protect themselves, and these can hurt those who feel excluded. Subjecting teenagers to adult authority always invites resistance, simply because that constitutes the developmental work of adolescence. Even with the best of intentions, a continual and trusting dialogue requires tension and struggle on both sides. Neither student nor teacher can afford to remain vulnerable, but both require vulnerability in order to do their jobs well.

When things go seriously wrong for students, many choose to stop going to school, sometimes for good. Teachers, too, make that choice when they feel discouraged—one reason that three out of five leave the profession in their first five years. Clearly, those choices hurt everybody in our society. How can we use the insights of students to understand and prevent them?

WHEN STUDENTS FEEL DISCOURAGED

Teenagers want to succeed in school, both socially and academically. When things go wrong in the first area, they often go wrong in the second, too.

> When I was first starting ninth grade I felt so alone. I used to cut every day, leave classes early, come in late, just to avoid being there. It was always about the people, not the academics. Some people like just being a face in the crowd, but it made me feel like nothing. VANCE

My ninth-grade year was tough. I was in a big school, probably the youngest, too, and not getting the attention I usually did. I didn't fit in because I felt too soft and new. School seemed like a fashion show for the kids, and a prison where the teachers were the wardens. I became an ordinary student; my average dropped and I couldn't figure out how. MIKA

Lacking the confidence and security of being known and appreciated, kids often falter in classes as well. They may feel overwhelmed by difficult new material, and afraid to make themselves conspicuous by asking for help.

I am one of the students that's in the crowd that teachers don't notice. I'm not liked and not disliked. It feels safer. I don't want to have people think I'm needy and I don't want to talk unless I'm sure I have the answer right. LAURALIZ

When their grades arrive, their confidence often suffers another blow.

I hurt when I get a bad grade! You feel like you're doing all that hard work for nothing. Then you don't want to work more, if you're just going to get bad grades. Whenever my grades get low I feel like dropping out of school. PORSCHE

You know you tried your best, and when you see your GPA is 1.57—I cried all day. It's sad when you're the first one in your family to graduate— they're waiting for you, and it's a lot of pressure. It's sad when you come up with a 1.57. VERONICA

To help prevent this devastating moment, students say, teachers should communicate with them early and often about how things are going.

> Once I had a math teacher and at the quarter almost no people had
> passed her test. So she gave us a questionnaire: How can I be a better
> teacher? What do you like or dislike about this class? How can I make it
> easier for you to learn? What was your weakness and strength in this
> class? MAHOGANY

One student group made the following list of questions for teachers to ask, before and after the report card:

BEFORE THE GRADING PERIOD ENDS, ASK:

How do you feel you are doing so far?

What things didn't you understand?

What should I have done differently?

What kinds of things helped you out this semester?

How can I help you now?

AFTER THE REPORT CARD ARRIVES, ASK:

How did this marking period go for you?

Do you think that's the grade you deserve? If not, why not?

What can you do to improve next time?

What can I as a teacher do better to help you?

SKIPPING SCHOOL AND DROPPING OUT

Students who don't feel noticed at school have a powerful temptation to stop going, especially if they think they can manage to pass their courses anyway.

> For ninth grade [my friend] was pretty good, but then the second half of the year she stopped going to school, but they kept her enrolled. She's only gone to school five days this whole year, and her grades are still passing. They don't know her! She'll show up—she showed up last week on Thursday and no one knew who she was. She was just there and then she left after lunch. DIANA

> My friend would only come to school close to report-card period, and then you wouldn't see him till the next report-card period. He would pass with Bs—he's smart, but it wasn't a challenge, and he would come for the final. Some teachers will do that: If you get an A on the final you get an A in the course. He was passing, and they never called his house.
> MAHOGANY

Especially in large and crowded high schools where teachers may have responsibility for as many as 150 students daily, checking up on attendance becomes an administrative task, not an expression of personal concern.

> When I was cutting school a lot they never called my house, until one of the security people who would see me told the attendance people. Then they called—but only because my mother said, "I want you to call me." DIANA

Lost in the crowd and often feeling excruciatingly alone, adolescent students may be protecting themselves from humiliation by staying home. A teacher's response can either allay that feeling or make it even worse.

I felt alone and uncomfortable, I was shy, so sometimes I wouldn't go. I was arrogant: I'm smart, I can do the work. After three straight days I went back and the teacher said in a sarcastic way, "Why are you here? I'm glad you've graced us with your presence." And that was it, I'm like: [forget] you. I just left and didn't go back. VANCE

[One of my teachers] makes tough decisions, but it's for the good. I feel like he's my coach. It matters to him whether I succeed or fail. He's rooting for me to graduate, to do good in classes, to be happy. MIKA

At the same time, teenagers know that leaving school ultimately hurts them. Even those who skip say they often try to use their time away from school to learn.

In my ninth-grade year I was at three big-ass schools in a row and I hated them all, so I stopped going. My mother took away my key so I couldn't go home, and so I started going to Barnes and Noble all day and just reading. I taught myself sign language from a book there. Like from September to March my record is nonexistent. ALEXIS

I went to the library, I would read, draw, be depressed. I knew: I should be in school, I'm alone, I'm stupid. Kids want to learn. VANCE

If no one intervenes, a teenager's days skipping school turn into a depressing spiral of failure.

When you skip school it's like an addiction, you skip it so much that you're like: What's the point of going, even if you want to be in the school. After a while it's not fun anymore, you're sitting there watching TV—all the stuff that was fun when you're first skipping gets a little boring. And you're like: I shoulda been in school, it would be more fun.

There's this block that keeps you from going. A kid knows their life is going down the drain. But if you don't like your school, and then you skip so much that you're embarrassed to go back, then you just don't go. I used to cut and smoke, and drink, and read. I think I was depressed. ALEXIS

Students tend to remember how adults respond in situations like this, and it matters to them.

My mom gets mad at that: So what if it's hard, it doesn't mean you have no chance! That's where people's personalities and drive come in. There's always an excuse—I could say I'm black, I'm poor, my mother abused me—but I could still do it. I know the system is set up in certain ways, but it's still possible. VANCE

If someone is going to say a smart-ass remark like, "Oh, you showed up today?" that in itself is going to make you not come back. [But] if I skip school and I go to [the principal] and tell him I skipped, I can ask, "Can you please not call my mom?" He respects that I told him, and he'll work it out. ALEXIS

WHEN TEACHERS FEEL DISCOURAGED

In their first year or two especially, teachers struggle to find the right balance between maintaining their authority and letting students know they care about them. Perhaps remembering their own years as students, they want to earn students' goodwill and win their cooperation. But sometimes that backfires.

Teachers think they're being understanding, but they're, like, false when they take it too far. We don't see being nice as such a good thing in a new teacher—you need to establish your authority. VANCE

When you're obviously new at this, kids are going to take advantage of you. You want to be liked so much that you're like: Okay, I won't give you homework today. ALEXIS

We would have did it, too! VANCE

Without giving up their human side, teachers have to put aside their fear and do the job, even as their teenaged students test them again and again.

We're just gonna crush your hope and pride. Teachers need to get a harder shell. After that, students won't see that you're scared. MIKA

My first-year teacher, the whole first semester we busted his chops, but then by second semester we let up on him, because we saw he was doing things right. Another teacher, we kept going on her because she was still scared. And kids go to the bathroom at times they're not supposed to, and then they set fires in the bathroom, while she was trying to be so friendly. LAURALIZ

Students will respond if a teacher comes to class prepared and confident. They know the bargain they are striking with good teachers, described in Chapter 2: Know and care about your material, treat us with respect and fairness, and we will pay attention, do the work, give up some of our freedom, and play by the rules.

The main thing is confidence. We're like dogs, we can sense fear and sniff it out. A kid can tell when a teacher knows what he's doing, and believes in what he's doing. Then they don't have to get into some authority struggle. VANCE

Don't let us intimidate you. When you let your student walk all over you, they're not learning the essentials of respect, of how to interact properly. Just be yourself, it's easier for students to gain something from you. Why can one teacher be respected and the other can't? It's confidence! If you project confidence, they won't attack. ALEXIS

Kids do want to learn, and they hate it just as much as teachers when classes become battlegrounds for control.

My new teacher spends half the time complaining and the other half trying to quiet the class down, while the rest of the class is waiting to learn something. LAURALIZ

WHAT TO TRY WHEN A CLASS GOES WRONG

Sometimes things deteriorate to a point where a teacher wants to throw in the towel altogether. Perhaps some class activity has bombed when kids behaved in unacceptable ways.

In my English class there's this kid who is really opinionated and argues with the teacher. We were reading Booker T. Washington, and he was arguing with other kids and going back and forth with the teacher. It felt unbalanced—it wasn't a respectful argument and the teacher didn't have control. She let it go on for too long. TIFFANY

Or perhaps in acting like a friend to students, the teacher has overstepped a delicate line.

Any time an adult goes too far because they want to get to know you, it happens. It's hard to go back and forth from being an authority to being a friend. To make a bond with your students you risk becoming too buddy-buddy. VANCE

Like everyone, teachers sometimes blunder or behave in insensitive ways.

During a band rehearsal our conductor was trying to tell the drummers to play more quietly, but they weren't listening to him and were continuing to play loudly. So the conductor shouted "We're not in Africa!" Several students in the band were offended by this statement, especially since he was a white conductor dealing with a majority of minority students. DARYL

Students have this advice for teachers discouraged by situations like these:

Don't be afraid to apologize.

The conductor recovered from it, because he was in general a nice guy, and none of the students had had racial problems with him in the past. The issue blew over; the students eventually forgave him for his comment and everything went back to normal. It would have been better if he had apologized right away, though. DARYL

Reexamine your teaching approach. Do students have a voice in setting behavior norms for the classroom? Do we understand why we are doing various class activities, and have you listened to our feedback?

[Teachers who lose the cooperation of the class] can try their best to get the respect of their class again. They can try things they didn't do before, things they know their students like. VERONICA

Don't take a bad day too hard. Every class period isn't a matter of life and death, and we know that too. Just as you give us second chances, we will do the same for you. Come back tomorrow, and next year.

> Relax and take your mind off school for a while. Think about the kids: We need you, we want to get out of school and become someone. [Try to] stay organized but relaxed. MONTOYA

Don't judge your success by whether students like you. We respect that your main job is to teach us. Do that well and the rest will follow.

> You really affect kids when you just do your job day in and day out, do it well—and everything doesn't have to be about bonding with the kids and changing their lives. That's artificial. The bond will develop on its own if you just do your job well. With a variety of personalities among teachers, a kid is guaranteed to connect with someone. VANCE

Don't try to be a superhero. No matter how much you care, you can't take responsibility for everything in kids' lives. And we don't expect you to.

> One problem with teachers is they want to be crusaders, they're so gung ho—"I'm going to go their house, together we can do that, Billy, together we can do it!" And then if that doesn't work they feel like failures, they get depressed because they didn't save that one kid, and so the twenty others suffer. Because all the energy is exerted on that one kid—you invest so much energy, and your drive, your determination, your love for the job is all spent on one student. VANCE

RECOVERING WHEN SOMETHING GOES WRONG: An Exercise for Teachers

Sometimes all it takes to make things better is thinking through what happened. When you feel as though something has gone wrong, try using this exercise to help get back to normal.

What happened?

_____

Who might have suffered from what happened?

_____

How might those people be feeling now?

_____

How are those people acting now?

_____

Can you think of a time when you suffered in a similar way from someone else's actions? If so, describe it here:

_____

Whose support do you need in order to make things better?

_____

What is the worst thing that could happen as a result of what went wrong?

_____

_____

Write down a plan for what actions you will take next.

_____

_____

DON'T GIVE UP ON KIDS

This most important piece of student advice deserves a section of its own. Teenagers know they sometimes drive their teachers crazy—they even take pleasure in it. But beneath that adolescent tendency lies a real hunger to form mutual and respectful partnerships with the adults in their lives. The following story, told by Veronica and analyzed by her Oakland classmates, speaks volumes about that complicated relationship.

> I think the teacher feels bad, too, when the students don't do their best. We had an algebra teacher, he was in a wheelchair. He was pretty nice but people took over him and screamed at him because he couldn't do anything about it. It was not nice because he was trying to help us. It was sad. He was depressed, he couldn't go on with the class. There was a whole month when we didn't do much.
>
> But after that we got to love him because he was nice. You couldn't judge a book by his cover. He changed some students' class, and then things started to get better. After that he talked about what happened to him—he had a bicycle accident and broke one of his disks. He used to try to make us laugh. He changed the whole class—he made us get involved. He won the respect of the class.

What did this teacher do right? Students answered that question without hesitation:

> He made the work more interesting. We would have groups with two persons at the board, one from the red team and one from the blue team. He would give us a problem and the team that solved it faster would win.

He changed the class assignments of certain students. They were supposed to be in geometry anyway.

He made himself human—talked about his accident, talked about his dreams of walking. Told us about his life in a way that made us understand him a little better.

He didn't give up on the students. We ended up learning.

Summary
WHEN THINGS GO WRONG

- **Don't be afraid to apologize.**

- **Reexamine your teaching approach.**

- **Don't take a bad day too hard.**

- **Don't judge your success by whether we like you.**

- **Don't try to be a superhero.**

- **Don't give up on us.**

CHAPTER 10

Going Beyond the Classroom

"IT WAS MORE FUN THAN IN THE CLASSROOM — AND WE LEARNED IT, TOO."

Especially for teenagers, school doesn't always provide the best setting for learning. At a time when adolescents want to try their wings, sitting in a classroom can feel frustratingly irrelevant and juvenile. They may not see the point of the subjects they must take or the importance of habits like punctuality and correct language. To get ideas about their own interests and potential, they often need inspiration from not just academic teachers but other adults doing related work.

Making connections with the world outside school addresses all these issues, and at the same time it usually helps students appreciate and value school more than they did before.

> That's the main way a teacher can keep hooks in the kids for longer—by connecting them to someone else who is a good person. So that even if you don't connect well to the student you can find someone who does. VANCE

> You want [kids] to find themselves, and not everyone is going to find themselves in the classroom. So you want to open as many doors as you can. LATIA

Some students are already learning a lot from their own families, as they take on growing responsibilities.

> I learned to fix things like lights and chairs from my uncle in Los Angeles. PEDRO

> Watching my younger brothers and sisters at home teaches me what
> having unprotected sex can lead to, if you are not ready for the responsi-
> bilities. And it was important for me to learn how to take care of them,
> so that I would know how when I have children. PORSCHE

But even more important, students say, are the learning opportunities that a thoughtful teacher can arrange outside their usual classroom routines. While kids almost always welcome such activities, they want them to have legitimate instructional value, too.

> If you're going to do an activity, make sure people really learn about
> something from it! We had to play dodgeball in science, to learn about
> mass and motion. VERONICA

> I didn't even know we were doing that! I thought we were just going to
> play dodgeball. LUIS

Student co-authors described several approaches that worked well for them.

Do regular class work outside the school. Many academic concepts come alive when presented in a context outside school. These opportunities can be as close by as the school yard or a neighborhood park, and involve no more expertise than what the teacher already possesses.

> In ninth-grade science, two times a week we went out to clean up a park
> with a pond in it. We learned about fish and their environment.
> MAHOGANY

> In biology we had to go outside and find a plant and measure it, draw it,
> see what kind of plant it was. That was good. When we were learning to

find the area and the perimeter in math, we went outside to measure the school. Also we had to go outside and find an angle, and draw what it was and measure its length and width. It was more fun than in the classroom—and we learned it, too. LUIS

In science class we walked for ten blocks to the park. We had to find examples around our community to show Maslow's hierarchy of needs. Like people playing soccer, that was an example of self-actualization. Transcendence was the mom pushing her baby, because she was willing to sacrifice something. We used the man driving a car to show physiological needs like water, oxygen, clothing, housing. That helped us remember. PORSCHE

Design projects that involve experts or other outside people for research or consultation.

For our final exam in English and world history we had a mock trial with a real judge and a court typist. They separated us into defense and prosecution, with four lawyers on each side, and they set up a mock scene from *Animal Farm* in which the character Boxer supposedly dies. The defense was defending the guy who supposedly killed him. We had to dress up and go down to City Center for three or four hours. It was pretty fun. We learned more about the book, but we also learned how to follow court procedures, write direct testimony, and do cross-examination. ANDRES

Try focusing on one extended learning experience outside the school. We particularly like learning experiences that take us out of our regular school-day routine, sometimes for longer time periods. This might mean going deeper into one topic for a week or more, or learning in several academic areas through a sustained experience or activity.

> Every year the week before spring break and after finals we have a "Week Without Walls." Every teacher comes up with a project, a total of twenty. They put up a list and you choose which one you want to do. In one week you get a whole quarter's worth of credit in whatever subject it relates to—like for camping, you can get 2.5 P.E. credits—so it's good for students who have fallen behind in their credits and need to make up. If you choose not to do it, you get five absent days, and of course you don't get the credit. ANDRES

> There's [a program] where you go for a semester and do survival skills and camping as well as take your classes. You get forty-five credits for the semester. MAHOGANY

Arrange internships for students. However modest our contribution, doing real work in a field that interests us not only develops new skills and habits but also gives us more motivation for academic work.

> In my acting internship, people come in with plays and one-act pieces. Once I saw what the others were doing, I realized I had something to contribute—you see other people, older or smarter, do something, and [it's] like, I can do this too! Last week I wrote a musical, like 25 minutes long, with text to hold it together. After I got positive feedback, it was easier to take criticism. They said: I liked this, but you could make this better. My teacher says that [the internship has] been good for me because I have problems with authority. Now my skills with that are better. I listen and take instructions better. I have responsibilities, I'm not on my own,

people depend on me for things, I have to answer the phone. There's a goal—at the end I'll be in a performance. I'm working on my play. You do these things, grunt work like cleaning the toilet, to work your way up the ladder, get skills. And your reward will be getting to do what you love. It's not going to come easy, but you learn that you have to do it. It gave me a better attitude toward school and homework—and toward life. It's more concrete now in my head. VANCE

Steer us toward summer and enrichment programs. Anything a teacher can do to keep us learning outside the school calendar pays off. What would you want your own kids to be doing when they weren't in school? Suggest it to us, too, and help us find ways to make it happen.

My neighbor told us about this radio and photography program aimed for high school students. You wrote a piece and put it on the air, and took a set of photos to go with it. I've done a lot of programs, like a math-science institute in [summer school] and another academic thing at City College. You could focus more on what you wanted. Each year you got something new that you liked or didn't like. LATIA

During Saturday classes I started learning more about little kids and what you can do with them and what you can't, and all sorts of other things about them. It was important for them to feel comfortable with me and trust me. DIANA

It helps to go away to camps, and school is a place where you can hook up with that kind of program, like leadership camp. You learn communication skills and you can be on your own. MAHOGANY

I went to youth camp—I had the greatest time in my life. I got to interact with kids younger than me, I got to sing, to make up a song—I want to do something like this! I want to wake up happy for a new day! I like to learn, I like to be productive. I want to test out every field I can. My mother wants me to get a job in a hospital and I want to learn photography. The school next door is a community college, and they offered our students to take courses there. LAURALIZ

Recognize and support our learning on our own. If we are doing something that interests us outside school, it's probably teaching us something. You may be able to connect to it somehow, and in any case your acknowledgment and respect matter to us.

I watch poetry readings, go to Barnes and Noble. Reading about new things interests me whenever I have spare time. I like knowing things or interesting facts that others don't know. I once taught myself sign language. ALEXIS

When I got involved with Youth in Action [a community action group] no one made me do that, I learned about it on my own. I always wanted to be involved in something like that. I felt it was important, reaching out to people my own age and younger, giving them knowledge. So many people my age have no idea how to protect themselves about STDs, HIV, etc. And I like writing grants for Youth in Action. It's an important skill to have. TIFFANY

HOW TO HELP STUDENTS LEARN OUTSIDE CLASS

Opportunities to stimulate students' interest in your academic area may be waiting just outside your school door. Use this exercise to make notes on the possibilities.

1. List a few important concepts or skills you would like your students to understand or develop.

_____

_____

_____

2. Choose any concept or skill from the list you made. Where outside school might someone be doing something that could not succeed without a grasp of that concept or skill? Write down every example you think of.

_____

_____

_____

3. Look over your list of examples. Do you see anything that might be taking place in a location close to school? If so, make note of all possibilities here, including specific contact information as you can obtain it.

_____

_____

4. Look over your answers from number 2. Can you imagine a student activity, project, internship, or enrichment experience that could connect to the people or resources you listed? Write any ideas here, even if they could not take place in a location near the school.

_____

_____

_____

5. Choose one of your ideas from number 4. What steps would you have to take to turn it into a reality?

_____

_____

_____

6. What additional resources do you need before proceeding?

_____

_____

_____

Summary

MOVING OUTSIDE THE CLASSROOM

- Take us outside the school regularly.

- Design projects that put us in touch with outside experts.

- Try one extended learning experience outside the school.

- Arrange internships for us.

- Steer us toward summer and enrichment programs.

- Recognize and support the learning we do on our own.

How We Wrote This Book—and Why It Matters

"HAS ANYONE EVER ASKED YOU QUESTIONS LIKE THIS BEFORE?"

Having adolescent students advise their own teachers often strikes educators and other adults as audacious. How can young people still in their teens be expected to summon the necessary know-how and perspective to help the adults charged with their very development and learning?

In fact, none of our student collaborators could answer in the affirmative when I queried, "Has anyone ever asked you questions like this before?" But for them, perhaps our project's most surprising aspect was how extraordinary it seemed to others.

Reflecting on how we developed its contents, in fact, I notice how much that process has in common with good teaching as this book describes it.

As every educator knows, good teaching entails far more than basic intelligence and knowledge. It requires the courage to look honestly at what is and imagine what it could be. It requires the humility to admit one's own mistakes and to keep trying. It requires empathy, to hear and feel what someone else is experiencing. And it takes genuine curiosity about people and ideas. In fact, good teaching looks a great deal like learning.

That insight provides a structure for anyone who wishes to expand understanding and improve practice by finding out what students have to say. The process I developed with What Kids Can Do, the organization that oversaw this project, involved these steps:

Come up with questions you really care about. We wanted to know what new teachers worried about most as they prepared to teach adolescents in diverse urban classrooms. So we began with that question. We asked several groups of beginning teachers, "What would you ask your students if you could ask them anything about what or how you teach?"

From their replies, we shaped at least a hundred questions, and sorted them into some thirty sets that seemed to go together. For example, new teachers expressed considerable anxiety about whether students would like them, and whether a friendly relationship would challenge their authority. So we decided to ask students to describe the teacher they liked the best, and also the teacher from whom they learned the most. Were those two different, and if so, why and how? We kept our questions concrete, basing them in the students' experiences and not just their opinions.

Not all of our questions bore fruit. Some, posed in language familiar to educators, met with blank stares from students. Other questions inadvertently took a perspective very different from that of students, implicitly asking them to conform their answers to our own assumptions. We learned to recognize the bombs, and to ask students, in the uncomfortable pauses: "Is this the right question? What do you think the real question is?" We continually asked students what questions we might be forgetting to ask. They acted as collaborators in the research, not as subjects, and their help framing and revising the questions immeasurably enriched what we learned.

Gather a group of students willing to express their thoughts. As the preface to this book describes, we used informal networks to recruit ordinary students who would make time to talk with us. Teenagers are busy people, and getting them together for sustained and serious work required the same persistence and respect that adults afford each other. We paid them for their time, for example, and provided good working conditions. But similar inquiries could also take place during school time, or as extracurricular projects. Getting adolescents to talk honestly takes only genuine interest in what they have to say.

Write everything down. Our sessions combined talking and writing, in a proportion that matched students' capacities and rhythms. Since we aimed to get at the important things no matter what it took, the facilitator used a laptop computer to record everything students said. We later transcribed their handwritten responses to our question sets as well.

That visible commitment to take account of everything students said created a powerful climate of serious purpose in our work sessions. At times, when students spoke too quickly or several students spoke at once, we had to slow them down and establish turns in order to keep up with the typing. A conversation that spiraled into casual jokes or personal chat tended to return more quickly to the subject as students saw their words written down. The facilitator often read back what people had said for accuracy, asking follow-up questions and giving them the chance to critique, amend, or amplify their comments.

At the same time, our sessions had a distinctly personal tone. Virtually everything kids said interested us: their individual styles and quirks, their personal stories and emotions, their problems and pressures, their frustration or excitement. Over breaks we shared food and, in those relaxed moments, our various worries or dreams as well. Kids got used to our saying, "Can you tell me more about that?" or "What was *that* like for you?" They could see that we regarded everything about them as important, and they gradually gave us their trust.

Ask for evidence. Kids are at least as ready as adults to spin out unfounded generalizations. So as they responded to questions, we continually sought supporting details. If they were speaking about the challenge of working in mixed groups, we pushed them to describe specific situations in which they had struggled or succeeded. If they complained about a teacher, we tried to nail down just how the teacher acted or spoke, not merely record the students' annoyance.

Inevitably inconsistencies emerged as they talked about their experiences and opinions, and so mining more details became their business, too. Yes, I do hate history, but in this one class we did something that made it more interesting. Teachers do use movies to hide when they're not prepared for class, but that one movie we saw made me think about things in a new way. We want teachers to act as if they like us, but if they're too nice, kids go off and set fires in the bathroom.

As students worked together, they grew more used to supporting their own assertions, and to probing each other's experiences for nuance and contradictions. The fact that we had to write something from their responses sharpened the need to get it right. They began to acquire the habits of the journalist and the researcher, looking always for pieces of the puzzle.

Analyze the material together. Since our book's goal was to offer advice, our discussions of students' experiences always ended with: "So what would you suggest to a teacher?" Analyzing the suggestions together, we created lists of Do's and Don'ts, calendars, questionnaires, and exercises to help teachers and students better understand each other. We weighed whether spontaneous advice ("We shouldn't have homework!") was merely frivolous or contained kernels of wisdom. Taken together, those analyses created much of this book's substance and dictated its organization.

Refreshingly, students' suggestions often derived from the example of a particularly effective teacher in their school. Again and again, kids testified to the power of a teacher to change not just their minds, but their lives. That pattern revealed another insight for those who would make schools better. Taking seriously students' evaluations of their teachers could help identify the masters among a faculty, and allow them to share their approaches with their colleagues.

Value the difference in perspectives. It's tempting to think that if you just pay attention to students' voices, you will hear what you already knew. After all, decades of experience have gone into shaping the way classrooms work, and these days a lot of wisdom and energy is going into making them better. Secretly, adults generally believe that they know best.

Of course, teenagers actually approach school from the vastly different perspective of their years. Their youth gives them license to scorn *Henry IV* as "the stupidest thing Shakespeare ever wrote," but they may accept as a given what their elders regard as controversial, like curriculum design or standardized tests. Knowing their futures may be decided on the basis of grades, they may value the grade far more than the learning in any particular class. They often feel like prisoners, fearing reprisal if they reveal weakness or speak the truth.

Even more important, the academic life of any teenager takes place within tumultuous personal change that typically overshadows all else. Making the transition to adulthood entails continual social and emotional risks as well as intellectual challenges, and school provides the dramatic arena for all these. Adults who focus on "student achievement" often forget that student learning consists of far more than subject-matter competence, extending to the critical relationships acted out between mentor and young person.

Our student collaborators' attention remained firmly on the same area that caused beginning teachers the most anxiety in our initial research. They saw school as a proving ground, with adults and students as the players. They wanted fairness and respect in that arena. They hungered for empathic attention to their individual needs. And they were willing to trade some freedom to get that crucial dignity.

Comparing that perspective to national education policy reveals a staggering disconnect.

Policy makers also cast high school as a proving ground, raising national standards as their banner and setting up frequent standardized tests as their sole measure of success. But rather than framing that proving ground as a unique challenge for every student, they force young people into a punitive system that sorts, selects, and often rejects them using one-size-fits-all measures.

Our systems emphasize control of student behavior, not dialogue in which students can participate and learn. "Zero tolerance" policies cancel out the possibility that making mistakes in adolescence can help a student move toward meaningful learning. Metal detectors at school doors send the message that they are passive captives, not responsible coconstructors of the school's culture.

School districts prize efficiency over every other aim. This results in large, factorylike high schools that stifle the opportunity for genuine relationships among students and teachers, or for imaginative classroom practices. Only when teachers can know their students well enough to respond to them individually will the suggestions in this book have any chance of taking root.

Finally, perhaps without intending to, our procedures shut out students from decisions about school structures and policies that affect them profoundly. This omission backfires in the end; students who feel disrespected can sabotage any initiative simply by not cooperating.

Students are not asking for total control over their education; they realize they have plenty to learn, and they crave contact with the adult world. But with all the national focus on standards and achievement, we often have forgotten that we are talking about young people who are developing as human beings. Unless we place at the top of our priorities their need to enter into meaningful partnerships with adults, their academic achievement will wither before it has a chance.

Listening to students does not depend on any particular expertise. Anyone who likes young people and values their opinions can do this work. It takes time, persistence, and attention to organize, but it could easily take place in the context of a classroom or advisory group. It requires thoughtful analysis to sort out patterns and draw conclusions from a flood of material, but educators and students possess those talents in abundance.

We offer our own questions as a place to start, but many more wait for future investigation. When we include such dialogue as a fundamental part of working with adolescents, we believe our education system will begin to fill up and spill over with the inspiration, energy, action, and learning that result.

Resources for Teachers

Teachers have hundreds of useful resources to call on, too many to name all of even the very best here. But for their sensitivity to the perspective of students, the following titles stand out. Each book offers suggestions for further reading as well.

William Ayers, *To Teach: The Journey of a Teacher* (New York: Teachers College Press, 2001)

John Bransford, Ann L. Brown, and Rodney R. Cocking, eds., *How People Learn: Brain, Mind, Experience, and School* (Washington, D.C.: National Academy Press, 2000)

Milhaly Csikszentmihalyi and Barbara Schneider, *Becoming Adult: How Teenagers Prepare for the World of Work* (New York: Basic Books, 2000)

Lisa Delpit, *Other People's Children: Cultural Conflict in the Classroom* (New York: The New Press, 1995)

Lisa Delpit and Joanne Kilgour Dowdy, eds., *The Skin That We Speak: Thoughts on Language and Culture in the Classroom* (New York: The New Press, 2002)

Robert L. Fried, *The Passionate Teacher* (Boston: Beacon Press, 1995)

Thomas Hine, *The Rise and Fall of the American Teenager* (New York: Harper-Collins, 2000)

Philip W. Jackson, *Life in Classrooms* (New York: Teachers College Press, 1990)

Philip W. Jackson, *The Practice of Teaching* (New York: Teachers College Press, 1986)

Herbert R. Kohl, *I Won't Learn from You: And Other Thoughts on Creative Maladjustment* (New York: The New Press, 1994)

Jonathon Kozol, *Savage Inequalities* (New York: HarperPerennial, 1992)

Gloria Ladson-Billings, *Crossing Over to Canaan: The Journey of New Teachers in Diverse Classrooms* (San Francisco: Jossey-Bass, 2001)

Gloria Ladson-Billings, *The Dreamkeepers: Successful Teachers of African-American Children* (San Francisco: Jossey-Bass, 1994)

Joseph P. McDonald, *Teaching: Making Sense of an Uncertain Craft* (New York: Teachers College Press, 1992)

Joseph P. McDonald, Nancy Mohr, Alan Dichter, and Beth McDonald, *Protocol Power: An Educator's Guide to Improving Practice* (New York: Teachers College Press, in press)

Deborah Meier, *The Power of Their Ideas: Lessons for America from a Small School in Harlem* (Boston: Beacon Press, 1995)

Jon Saphier and Robert Gower, *The Skillful Teacher* (Carlisle, MA: Research for Better Teaching, 1987)

Theodore R. Sizer, *Horace's Compromise: The Dilemma of the American High School* (Boston: Mariner Books, 1997)

Theodore R. Sizer and Nancy Faust Sizer, *The Students Are Watching: Schools and the Moral Contract* (Boston: Beacon Press, 1999)

Beverly Daniel Tatum, *"Why Are All the Black Kids Sitting Together in the Cafeteria?" And Other Conversations About Race* (New York: Basic Books, 1999)

Acknowledgments

Though this book owes its strength largely to its student collaborators, *Fires in the Bathroom* would never have come about without the imagination, persistence, and generosity of many others. Foremost among them is MetLife Foundation, whose findings in *The MetLife Survey of the American Teacher* indicated that teachers feel less than prepared to work with students from language, ethnic, or racial backgrounds different from their own and have little knowledge of their students' neighborhoods and communities. Hoping to give voice to students and provide a resource for teachers, MetLife Foundation suggested the project to What Kids Can Do, a nonprofit organization dedicated to making public the work and learning of adolescents. Within weeks, the book's research began, supported by a MetLife grant.

Interest at The New Press followed close behind, with the initial support of education editor Maureen Grolnick, a former high school teacher and principal who brought the book to the attention of Executive Director Diane Wachtell. We owe deep appreciation not only to Diane for her quick understanding of the book's importance, but also to her assistant, Beth Slovic, who facilitated the endless tasks along the way. Ellen Gordon Reeves returned to The New Press as education editor just in time to provide her thoughtful editorial guidance once the manuscript was ready. Maury Botton gave perceptive guidance to the book's production, and Miles Norton and Julie McCarroll to its marketing and publicity; we are indebted to them for their generous and collaborative spirit. Sandra Delany brought the book's complex elements into an elegant type design in unusually difficult circumstances, with invaluable help from Kelly Gould.

Before work with high school collaborators began, gathering the perspectives and worries of beginning teachers was essential. We owe tremendous appreciation to the education faculties of four universities in the cities from which we drew our student co-authors. At Brown University in Providence, clinical professors Bil Johnson, Eileen Landay, and Larry Wakeford made possible hours of conversation with students who were about to teach in secondary schools, including Daniel Filler, Ryan Foote, Shivohn Garcia, Kristen Graham, Chris Magnuson, Jennifer Mitnick, Melissa Mock, Erin Northey, Judy Ritten, John Roby, Melissa Schoeplein, Sam Seidel, Laura Shaw, and Cherise West. At New York University, faculty members Joe McDonald, Tony Cavanna, Robbie Cohen, and Cynthia L. Shor brought pizza and wisdom to conversations with new teachers Sue Marie Soto, Barbara Hull, Dusty Fox, Patricia O'Rourke, Carolina Bermudez, and Sarah Gil, among others. At Stanford University's Teacher Education Program, Rachel Lotán helped us obtain feedback from her students Maureen Chang, Treena Joi, Amanda Day, Danielle Wright, and Kara Mitchell at a particularly crucial point in the manuscript's development. And Herb Kohl, who directs the teacher preparation program at University of San Francisco, also offered his support.

Finding and gathering high school students willing to devote many hours of thoughtful work to the book could not have happened without the generous help of several dedicated teachers and organizations. Enormously helpful in this task was Summerbridge, a national organization (now changing its name to the Breakthrough Collaborative) that prepares urban youngsters to succeed in high school academics through the coaching of older students from high school and college. In Providence, Summerbridge directors Mindy Weber and Jay Huguley not only located student collaborators but also provided space for us to work at its Wheeler School offices. At Manhattan Summerbridge, Sam Marks helped us reach out to New York City students, as did San Francisco Summerbridge director Carolina Martín in the Bay Area. In addition, researcher

Becky Crowe and Nicolette Toussaint at the Bay Area School Reform Collaborative not only helped us find students but also lent us the BASRC offices for several long days of student work sessions. In Oakland, the help of Kathy Simon and Sara Rubin at the Coalition of Essential Schools led us to our excellent working space at the East Bay Community Foundation's conference center.

Just as important were the high school teachers who suggested students to work with us. In the Bay Area, Laura Flaxman at Life Academy in Oakland, Laura Kretschmar at the Lighthouse School, Seewan Eng at San Francisco Community School, Gia Truong at Leadership Academy, and Cheryl Lana at Thurgood Marshall Academic High School helped us locate students. In an enormously generous contribution, teacher Patricia Chandler at El Cerrito High School opened her English Language Development class to us for three days of intensive conversation with students. Ann Cook, at Urban Academy in New York City, put us in touch with several students who became key collaborators.

As the manuscript took shape, several seasoned teachers lent their sharp eyes and wise perspectives by reading drafts of the manuscript. Invaluable critiques came especially from Rob Riordan, Seewan Eng, and Bil Johnson; John R. Bohannon, Sr. also contributed teaching techniques that enriched our suggestions.

During the final stages of synthesis and writing, Eliza C. Miller gave many hours to organizing students' commentary and helping frame the chapters that resulted. Lisa Rowley, a masterful editor at What Kids Can Do, Inc., put the manuscript through her fine-tooth comb before it went to The New Press.

From start to finish, I owe my deepest thanks to Barbara Cervone, the founder and president of What Kids Can Do, Inc. Her staunch support, indefatigable energy, and fierce intellect sustained me through every difficulty. My three remarkable daughters, Montana, Eliza, and Rosa Carolina, picked up where she left off, teaching me firsthand, as always, what kids can do.

Brief Biographies

Note: Students' ages and locations are given as of the time of their collaboration, in spring 2002.

Alexis, 18, was born and raised in New York and attends a small public high school in Manhattan.

Andres, 15, grew up in San Francisco, where he attends a small public high school.

Bosung, 16, was born in New York and grew up in Providence, Rhode Island, where he attends public high school and teaches younger students in the Summerbridge program.

Daryl, 17, grew up in Providence and attends an independent school there. He teaches middle school students in the Providence Summerbridge program.

Diana, 15, was born in Nicaragua and moved to San Francisco, where she attends public high school.

Hilary, 19, was born and raised in Palo Alto, California. A participant in the San Francisco Summerbridge program, she attends the University of California at Berkeley.

Latia, 17, was born and brought up in New York City, where she attends a small high school and participates in the Manhattan Summerbridge Program.

Lauraliz, 17, was born in Puerto Rico and moved as a child to the Bronx, where she attends a large public high school.

Luis, 16, was born in Mexico and grew up in Oakland, where he goes to high school.

 Mahogany, 17, grew up in San Francisco and attends a small public high school there.

 Maribel, 16, attends a large public high school in Providence, Rhode Island; she has also lived in New York City, Miami, and the Dominican Republic. She teaches younger students in the Providence Summerbridge program.

 Mika, 16, came to New York from Jamaica at age four. She lives in the Bronx and attends a small Manhattan public school.

 Montoya, 16, grew up in Oakland, California and attends a small public high school there.

Nathan, 18, grew up in Lexington, Massachusetts and attended public schools there.

 Porsche, 16, was born and raised in the San Francisco Bay area and goes to high school in Oakland, where she lives.

 Sandy, 17, lived in New York until 1996, then moved to Providence, Rhode Island, where she attends a large public high school. She has participated in Providence Summerbridge.

 Tiffany, 16, was born and raised in Providence, Rhode Island, where she attends an independent school and teaches younger students in the Summerbridge program.

 Vance, 18, was born and raised in Harlem and attended several New York City high schools.

 Veronica, 15, was born and raised in Oakland, California, where she now attends a small public high school.

The class of English-language learners and their countries of origin:

Karen, 16 (Hong Kong)

Elaine, 16 (Brazil)

Donnel, 15 (Philippines)

Nai, 14 (Thailand)

Barbara, 16 (Chile)

Tsugumi, 15 (Japan)

Javier, 17 (Mexico)

Yuri, 15 (Peru)

Rafael, 16 (Peru)

Krishneel, 15 (India)

Ximena, 15 (Peru)

Pedro, 16 (Mexico)

Murilo, 14 (Brazil)

Luciana, 17 (Brazil)

Cynthia, 15 (Guatemala)

Jae, 15 (Korea)

Samuel, 14 (Japan)

Marcos, 15 (Brazil)

Jin Fen, 16 (China)

Kirandeep, 15 (India)

Brian (China)

Index